Arate £3—

BAYWATCH™

ALL AMERICAN TELEVISION ACKNOWLEDGEMENT

After twenty-two weeks on NBC, Baywatch was pulled from the schedule. While the network cited marginal ratings, what they failed to recognize was that a quiet yet fiercely loyal core of fans – both in the United States and overseas – had bonded with David Hasselhoff and the cast. Fortunately, a newly formed and aggressive independent production and distribution company realized the series' potential.

All American Television, headed by global entertainment entrepreneur Anthony Scotti, seized the opportunity to arrange for the production and financing of the show. David Hasselhoff and the show's original production team were brought back on board and an agreement was reached so that Baywatch would go back into production and be sold market by market to individual stations in the United States and worldwide.

Within weeks, the cameras were rolling again at Will Rogers State Beach near Santa Monica. Baywatch, a series celebrating the heroics of lifeguards, had been rescued.

EXECUTIVE PRODUCER ACKNOWLEDGEMENTS

This book is possible because of the vision of four people whose creativity, single-minded determination, and will to succeed resulted in the worldwide entertainment phenomenon known as Baywatch. In 1989, after seeing their first season of Baywatch end in network cancellation, Michael Berk, Douglas Schwartz, Gregory J. Bonann, and David Hasselhoff formed their own production company outside of the traditional studio system and gave Baywatch a second life in first-run syndication. It took over fourteen months to finalize the necessary distribution agreements with domestic television stations and international licensees, but in July of 1991, Baywatch began filming again in Malibu, California. In the years since, the series has exploded across the international and domestic scene, but always under the close supervision of the four visionaries who nurtured it back to life.

Co-creators and executive producers, Michael Berk and Douglas Schwartz, are first-cousins who have been making movies together since their pre-teens. With over forty-five years' combined experience as writer/producer/directors, Michael and Doug's solid track record in television enabled them to sell Baywatch to Grant Tinker and NBC in 1988. Prior to creating Baywatch, they wrote and produced fifteen award-winning TV movies including the critically acclaimed *The Ordeal of Dr Mudd* and *The Haunting Passion*. They have been nominated for two Emmy awards and in 1987 created the ground-breaking television series, *The Wizard*. Michael is the principal scriptwriter on Baywatch, having penned the pilot and over thirty episodes, in addition to directing five episodes. Douglas has directed over thirty episodes, including the first-ever Baywatch movie, *Forbidden Paradise*, and has co-written over fifteen episodes.

Gregory J. Bonann, co-creator/executive producer, is a veteran LA county lifeguard, Medal of Valor winner, and award-winning documentary filmmaker who memorialized the Olympic games on film in 1980, 1984, and 1988. Greg has directed over thirty episodes of Baywatch and is the driving creative force behind the signature Baywatch montage and action sequences.

Executive Producer and series star, David Hasselhoff, began his acting career at age seven performing neighborhood theater in Atlanta, Georgia. Hasselhoff first caught the attention of American television viewers in 1975 when he was cast as Snapper Foster in the perennial soap-opera hit *Young and The Restless*. After seven seasons of soaps, David starred in the hit NBC prime time television series *KnightRider* as Michael Knight, a role which brought him international fame and launched his very successful international recording career. He has released six albums in Europe and just released his self-titled seventh album in the US. Known as one of the most bankable international actors working in film and television, David, along with Greg, Doug, and Michael, just created the eagerly anticipated Baywatch spin-off series, *Baywatch Nights*.

BAYWATCH™

THE INSIDE STORY

DEBORAH SCHWARTZ

MICHAEL JOSEPH

LONDON

MICHAEL JOSEPH LTD

Published by the Penguin Group
27 Wrights Lane, London W8 5TZ
Viking Penguin Inc., 375 Hudson Street,
New York, New York 10014, USA
Penguin Books Australia Ltd, Ringwood,
Victoria, Australia
Penguin Books Canada Ltd, 10 Alcorn
Avenue, Toronto, Ontario, Canada M4V 3B2
Penguin Books (NZ) Ltd, 182-190 Wairau
Road, Auckland 10, New Zealand

Penguin Books Ltd, Registered Offices:
Harmondsworth, Middlesex, England

First published 1995
Copyright © Deborah Schwartz 1995
BAYWATCH™ and logo TM & © 1995
The Baywatch Production Company

Typeset in Bodoni
Design: Design/Section, Frome
Printed in Great Britain by
Butler & Tanner Ltd, Frome and London

A CIP catalogue record for this book is
available from the British Library

ISBN 0 7181 4117 2

The moral right of the author has been
asserted

Photographers' Acknowledgements
Kim Carlsberg's ocean and lifeguard
photography inspired the creation of
this book. As the original Baywatch
still photographer and the principal
photographer for the first two seasons
of production, Kim's artistry has shaped
the public's perception of Baywatch in
advertisements, posters, calendars,
and press articles over the years.
Other photographers whose work is
featured in the following pages include:
Danny Feld, Spike Nannerello, Joe Viles,
Stanley Newton.

Contents

Introduction

Baywatch is more than just a television show, it is a way of life . . . a dream lifestyle. It is the magic of the sun, the surf, the slow-motion beauty of the music montages, the sparkle on the water and the sparkle in Mitch Buchannon's eye, as he and his family of drop-dead gorgeous women lifeguards and Adonis-type male lifeguards watch their water and guard the beautiful people who come to enjoy the beach. One billion people in over 142 countries escape to enjoy Baywatch every week. In fact, in the USA, this sun-soaked escape now takes place on a daily basis as Baywatch airs encore shows of the over 100 episodes previously produced.

Hailed as "the most popular TV series in the history of the planet", one thing is certain, whether it is David Hasselhoff's character, Mitch Buchannon, whose moral courage, vulnerability and heroism put him up there with the likes of John Wayne, the stories that pull at your heart strings, or the hunks in trunks and the babes in bikinis – Baywatch is a mega hit. Quite an accomplishment for any television show.

In 1988, Baywatch was originally developed as a pilot movie for a series by NBC. Its successful ratings earned Baywatch a place as a series on NBC's 1989 fall line-up. At the end of the season, however, NBC cancelled the show because they didn't believe that a show featuring lifeguard rescues every week would last. What no one recognized, except the show's executive producers, Michael Berk, Douglas Schwartz, Gregory Bonann, and David Hasselhoff, was that Baywatch wasn't just about the rescues and CPR; it was also about the lives of the characters and their relationships. That and the California lifestyle are what the show is about.

It took the executive producers one year to give Baywatch mouth-to-mouth resuscitation and bring it back to life in first-run syndication.

All American Communications, an aggressive television production and distribution company, believed that Baywatch had the potential to catch on, and sold Baywatch, television station by television station, across the country. It is now cleared in over ninety-five per cent of the United States.

Baywatch returned to the air in the fall of 1991 in first-run syndication in the United States as well as airing in twenty countries around the world, due in large part to David Hasselhoff's international fame. By its fifth anniversary since cancellation by NBC, Baywatch had become a legend, regularly viewed by over one billion people in 142 countries. At last count, there were only 189 countries in the world, so Baywatch still has some fans to win over. Shouldn't take long!

Baywatch is often criticized because it is not reality. True and not true. Take it from me, the stories I write come out of my head, from my imagination. But these stories are often based on everyday reality. For instance, what it is like for a dwarf to have a full-sized son, or what it is like for an obese girl to sit on the beach surrounded by a bevy of perfect bodies, or a son to deal with his mother who has developed Alzheimer's disease. And what could be more reality based than a child pulling his unconscious

brother from the swimming pool and giving him mouth-to-mouth resuscitation because he had seen accurate CPR techniques on Baywatch! Even lifeguards now like the show. As David Hasselhoff says, "At first they were skeptical . . . but lifeguards from all over the country were coming up to me and going, 'Hey man, thanks. Everybody respects our profession now and knows we aren't just guys who are checking out babes at the beach.'" What more could you ask for?

Of course Baywatch is filled with the fantasy lifestyle. After all, it is not a documentary. "I think Baywatch gives people a great escape," says Pamela Anderson. French-born actor David Charvet, who spent three seasons as Baywatch's moody lifeguard Matt Brody, says, "Hollywood . . . is where the stars come from . . . the beaches and the palm trees. That whole fantasy is so realistic to the Europeans."

Popular television shows like *Ozzie and Harriet*, *Father Knows Best*, and *Dynasty* were not reality based. But they were hits because they allowed the viewing public to escape and relax – something we all need. Consider it free therapy, if you will. There is nothing wrong with admitting that one likes to escape, relax and fantasize. It is not always possible for people to get away to the beach where the water is cool and blue, the sun is warm, and the bodies are bronze. But once a week, viewers from around the world can enjoy a one-hour holiday by tuning into Baywatch.

Even so, United States viewers are more reluctant to admit their addiction to Baywatch than the European audience. Well, maybe we should start Baywatch Anonymous, and each member could begin by standing up and announcing that he or she is a Baywatch devotee. Slowly, Baywatch viewers are coming out of the closet, proud to announce that they are fans of Baywatch because they love the show. One billion viewers would agree.

Why is Baywatch so popular around the world? By combining heroic action with music montages, beautiful people, lovable characters, and David Hasselhoff's immense popularity, the executive producers and producers of Baywatch have created a product with universal appeal. They have hit on a formula for selling "The American Dream". Douglas Schwartz and Michael Berk, co-creators and executive producers, believe Baywatch is one of the only shows on television that blends together action, adventure, heart-warming stories, MTV-style music videos, strong character relationships, wholesome family values and a group of dedicated lifeguards who are heroes saving lives every day. It isn't any one aspect then that makes the show a hit, but a blending of aspects. Because of this, the show appeals to a very broad audience, which includes families watching the show together. What does executive producer and star David Hasselhoff think the answer is to the question of Baywatch's popularity? "It's the California lifestyle . . . what the Beach Boys made famous . . . this is what they think California is like," says Hasselhoff.

Voted the world's most popular male star, David Hasselhoff heads up the cast of Baywatch. His well-muscled, charismatically handsome alter ego, Mitch Buchannon, is the epitome of one handsome hunk of a southern California lifeguard. Add to that his responsibility as a single father, and his abundant charm, and it is hard to top him. But there is nothing disgraceful about being second best to Mitch Buchannon, lifeguard extraordinaire. When the hunky lifeguards are not busy pulling people out of the sea like tuna, they will be at each others' throats — off duty of course. Over what? Beautiful women, what else?

"I wish they all could be California girls . . . " Since Baywatch's inception, there has been a procession of beautiful California blondes across our screens. But no one has personified the California beach-blonde image more than Canadian-bred Pamela Anderson. "I think there is a mystery about California that everybody in the world is drawn to . . . One of my ambitions was always just to get to California and see a palm tree," says Pamela. Well, Pamela certainly exceeded her goal. Without question, she has become the sexiest, hottest and most popular woman on television today, via her role as CJ Parker on Baywatch, unable to make a move without causing a stir.

During its first year on NBC, Lifeguard Headquarters was built on a soundstage with a backdrop of a painted ocean. In order to make it look realistic, scotch tape was dotted on the

painted water and then blown with a fan to get that shimmer effect of sunlight on the water. All in all, not a great effect. Thus, when preparing for the first season for syndication, the L.A. County Lifeguard Association gave the executive producers permission to build the lifeguard headquarters set for Baywatch above the real lifeguard headquarters at Will Rogers beach. Now, the backdrop became the real ocean, the real beach — and even the real lifeguards. While the lower floor of headquarters houses the genuine lifeguards, responding to emergencies all day long, the upper floor houses the actor lifeguards. No other film company, whether it be for a cop show, detective show or medical show, has ever built their set on top of the real-life headquarters.

I was born and raised in southern California. As a child, I played in the surf at Will Rogers, Santa Monica and Malibu beaches. As a teenager, my brother became a lifeguard, and for many years lifeguards and lifeguarding became my world. The lifeguards were my friends as well as my heroes. Whether I was attending their lifeguard competitions and cheering them on, bringing them cake to their lifeguard towers, or working out with them in the pool, they were heroes to me. And they are still my life now. Working with them and writing about them is my job, my life. So I bring this book to you from the inside. The inside world of Baywatch, the inside world of lifeguarding . . . Baywatch, the inside story.

Deborah Schwartz

Mitch Buchannon

David HASSELHOFF

David Hasselhoff on Mitch Buchannon: "Mitch has had a lot of losses in his life. He lost a close relationship with his father because he chose to be a lifeguard, then his dad died. He lost his wife Gayle because of his dedication to his career, and came close to losing Hobie several times when Gayle sued for custody. Mitch and his brother Buzzy had a falling out and he no longer sees him. His close friend Jill Riley was killed by a shark while rescuing a child, Al Gibson, his surrogate father, died while making a heroic rescue, Stephanie dumped him to return to her ex-husband who Mitch didn't know existed, and his best friend John Cort was going blind and left town, and when Mitch finally met and fell in love with Tracy, the woman of his dreams, she died of cancer.

Now Mitch's mother has developed Alzheimer's disease and he has to face that inevitable loss. Frankly, I don't know how the guy keeps going. But he does, because he is . . . Mitch Baywatch. Mitch Buchannon reminds me of myself. No matter what happens, he's still standing.

Being a lifeguard has proved very costly for Mitch Buchannon. It cost him his relationship with his father, who wanted Mitch to join him in his architectural firm. It also cost him his marriage to Gayle, and almost his son Hobie. But Mitch just made lieutenant, and he's not so sure he likes wearing the hard-soled shoes, or, as Ben calls them, "the crab stompers". He feels he's more cut out to be on the sand, nearer the action.

This is the exact kind of thing that drives his ex-wife Gayle nuts. Gayle thinks Mitch needs to grow up and get a real job. Mitch tells her she doesn't understand lifeguarding. He believes there could be no more real job than saving people's lives – what is more important? Gayle tells her ex-husband that, in her opinion, he'd rather save lives twenty-four hours a day than save their marriage. Gayle informs Mitch that she can't allow Hobie to live with him and be influenced this way. Hobie needs consistency. Gayle's job as head of marketing for a restaurant chain is transferring her to Ohio, and she intends to sue for full custody of Hobie, taking him with her. Mitch is heartbroken.

But Gayle comes to see the error of her ways. When she discovers how much Hobie loves his dad and needs to be with him, she decides not to take him away from Mitch after all. Mitch realizes he will always love this woman. Years later they almost remarry, but Mitch stands Gayle up at the altar in order to save many lives after a fishing boat catches fire. Mitch's decision just reinforces for Gayle that his lifeguarding commitment will always come before her.

Mitch's lifeguarding continued to be a major source of conflict with his father right up until he died. His mother Irene is always supportive, only caring about Mitch's happiness. When she is diagnosed with Alzheimer's disease, Mitch is devastated. But his spunky mother, determined to let

nothing get her down, decides to take advantage of the time she has left in this short life. She begins by travelling through Europe with her bridge group who will look after her.

Raising Hobie comes first for Mitch, which manages to limit his social life somewhat. But he has had a variety of women in his life. Besides his affair with Stephanie Holden, Gayle returning to his life, and a few other dates in between, Mitch falls for a girl he rescues who claims she has seen a sea monster. He gets involved with two sisters, complete opposites, who turn out to be one woman with a multiple personality disorder. The "bad" personality tries to kill him, but Mitch saves his own life by reasoning with the "good" personality. He gets involved with a woman who, unbeknownst to him, is a princess and is the target of an assassination plot. And a girl he saved in his rookie days returns years later to claim her hero Mitch as her own. She has never forgotten him. Of course, her fiancé is not so thrilled . . .

But the day Mitch meets beautiful, blonde Aussie, Tracy, a hovercraft rescue expert, he learns the true meaning of being in love. When Mitch finally proposes to the woman of his dreams, she turns him down. He doesn't understand until she reveals to him that she is dying. A heartbroken Mitch holds Tracy in his arms at their favorite spot overlooking the ocean at sunset, and she silently leaves this world.

Mitch is the epitome of a heroic lifeguard. He has risked his life on many occasions to make a presumably impossible rescue. He has made over one thousand rescues during his career, and never lost a victim. Many of his rescues have become legendary. After rescuing a diver trapped ninety feet below the surface of the ocean, Mitch almost dies himself from decompression sickness.

While rescuing three panicked teenagers trapped on dangerously jagged rocks in crashing surf, Mitch breaks his back and faces paralysis. He flashes back to the day fellow lifeguard and best friend Eric Turner broke his back while rescuing a teammate during a competition. Eric never recovered the use of his legs, and Mitch inspired him to stop feeling sorry for himself. Now Mitch faces the same fate. Everyone at Baywatch misses him terribly while he is in hospital, and they all sit around hoping to cheer one another up by reminiscing about the day Mitch called in a rescue that turned out to be a paper bag. When Mitch went into the shower room after his day's work, all the guys in the shower beckoned to Mitch for help . . . with paper bags on their heads! Following painful physical therapy, and with a great deal of determination, Mitch recovers the use of his legs while rescuing an inner-city boy whom the Mafia is trying to eliminate because he witnessed a drug-related gang killing. After Mitch saves the boy, he returns to Baywatch and lifeguarding.

Mitch's two best female friends are Stephanie Holden and CJ Parker. Mitch finds himself in the middle when they both compete for a starring role in *Rescue Bay*, a new television series starring . . . Mitch Buchannon. When the two girls argue over who is best suited for the role, Mitch agrees to read a love scene with each of them, starting a jealous love match between Stephanie and CJ. Mitch is in a predicament. He loves them both, and they're both terrific kissers. As luck would have it, the whole project dies. But Mitch never forgot those love scenes . . .

Mitch and CJ have been friends for years. Mitch looked after CJ as if she were his little sister during her rookie year as a lifeguard. He has seen her through many disastrous love affairs, and felt his loyalties torn between CJ and Cort when they broke up. Mitch eventually finds himself thinking amorous thoughts about CJ, and when she confides in Mitch, he finds himself having to keep CJ's very deep secret as he wrestles with his mounting romantic feelings.

Deserving a little perk, Mitch and the other guards have an opportunity to go to Hawaii to work with some of the best lifeguards in the world. On their free weekend, Matt and Mitch go diving off a remote island. When Matt is stung by a poisonous fish, Mitch has to carry a weakened Matt through the jungle, rescue him when he falls off a waterfall, and battle unfriendly natives who are after them. Just another day in paradise.

Mitch Buchannon, the heart and soul, the pulse of Baywatch, is a lifeguard's lifeguard. Mitch is someone who doesn't present himself as being a better lifeguard than the others . . . he just is. This special quality endears him to all the other lifeguards who look up to and respect Mitch. He is the leader, the pied piper of Baywatch headquarters, looking out for and guiding his fellow lifeguards. Mitch Buchannon is the man to measure the race by.

Hobie Buchannon

JEREMY JACKSON

Jeremy Jackson on Hobie Buchannon: " Hobie is torn between his music and wanting to be a lifeguard. He is also torn between his mom and dad. Even though he is getting older, and as much as he loves his dad, he really misses having a mom. Also, Hobie gets a little too emotional sometimes."

Hobie Buchannon lives the fantasy life of every kid . . . his dad's office is the beach. But even though Hobie gets to spend a lot of his time on the sand and in the surf, he has problems with parents, school and friends – just like every other kid.

When his parents divorce and his mother moves to Ohio, he misses her, but he has a special bond with his dad that cannot be equaled. When Hobie's mother, Gayle, comes out to visit with Ken, her wealthy fiancé, Mitch is a little jealous of Ken and all he can offer Hobie. Gayle surprises Mitch with her plan for Hobie to come and live with her and Ken when they are married.

Their plans to fly to Acapulco with Hobie for the wedding are brought to an abrupt halt when Ken's private plane crashes into the ocean, trapping them all underwater. Hobie heroically risks his own life to save his mother when Ken proves to be a coward. In a race against time, Mitch rescues them all, but Hobie and Mitch never tell Gayle about Ken's cowardice. Realizing Hobie should be with his father, Gayle decides not to take him with her and, eventually, she cancels her plans to marry Ken.

When an earthquake hits California, Hobie, who almost loses his life when a beam falls on him in the garage, chooses to move to Ohio to live with his mother.

This arrangement does not last long, and he is soon back home in California working on his music and playing in his band. Hobie is very active in junior lifeguards, an organization where kids and teenagers learn all about ocean safety and how to become lifeguards.

Even though Hobie has so much exposure to lifeguarding, his true love is music. Mitch encourages him to follow his dream, something his own father never allowed him to do. But when Mitch finds out that Hobie idolizes Johnny Danger, a daredevil stuntman who also drinks way too much, there is nothing he can do until Hobie's friends drink beer and one of them almost drowns. They all get a big lecture from Mitch. Hobie learns a lesson about who is worthy of idolizing when a drunken Johnny drives his motorcycle off the end of the pier.

Like many teenagers, Hobie does some dumb things in order to find acceptance. When he tells a lie to impress a pretty girl, the lie comes back to haunt him when some rough kids, thinking Hobie knows something he really doesn't, threaten to beat him up if he tells anyone else. The next time Hobie gets a crush on a girl, he doesn't care about impressing her.

The love bug bites again when Hobie meets Lauren, a girl in junior lifeguards. What Hobie doesn't know is that Lauren has been brought to town by the make-a-wish foundation, a foundation that grants wishes to terminally ill children.

Hobie and Lauren share a few days of love and lifeguarding, until Hobie has to rescue a weakened Lauren during a swim. Lauren's parents, fearing all the activity is too much for her, take her home.

Hobie learns an invaluable lesson about friendship when he meets and befriends Manny, an eight-foot giant who works in a sideshow on the pier. Manny is mistreated by his manager, and Hobie teaches him that he can be whatever he wants and do whatever he wants – including having fun. Hobie helps Manny realize his dream of becoming a sculptor and opening his own shop on the pier.

With all the friends Hobie has had and still has, his best friend remains, through thick and thin, his dad. Mitch has been both mother and father to Hobie over the last six years, creating a very special bond. Hobie doesn't want to let his dad down by making the wrong choices, and Mitch doesn't want to let his son down by not being there for him. They have made a pact that each will always tell the other his true feelings . . . no matter how painful.

Hobie is faced with a different set of problems now that he is older. He used to get into trouble by succumbing to peer pressure, but now makes better choices for himself, based on right and wrong and what he wants, not what others want. Instead of being a follower, Hobie has become a leader, like his father, and has matured into a young man with an eye for the ladies. Hobie's love life is taking off and he is beginning to experience the trials and tribulations that come with all relationships.

Not just a day at the beach

The sun comes up, spilling its jeweled light across the blue ocean water, creating sparkling waves that roll gently to shore. The summer sand is cool and quiet, the lifeguard towers unopened. The only signs of life are the sea gulls that swoop and call to one another, a school of dolphins playing in the glistening waves as they head up the coast, and a family of seals overlapping one another as they all try to snooze on one buoy anchored offshore. For the few joggers who may be out for a run at dawn, the solitary experience of these early-morning sights along with the sounds of the crashing surf, the spray of the sea, and the feel of the ocean breeze, are a far cry from the beach scene that will unfold as the sun rises, along with the temperature, and southern Californians head for the beach. They come to the beach to walk, to think, to romance, to play, to picnic, to exercise, to enjoy. People like to ride their bikes, walk, or roller-blade along the bike path that winds along the sand from Santa Monica as far south as Redondo beach. It is a beautiful ride or walk with the beach and the ocean at your side.

Surfers load their boards in their vans and head for Malibu or Huntington beach to catch the waves. Families pack up their lunches, grab their umbrellas, their sunblock and their kids and head for their favorite beach. By the time thousands of beachgoers arrive and set up along the seventy-three miles of sand, L.A. county lifeguards are set up in their towers, their hands full with everything from water rescues to bee stings to lost children. Lifeguard trucks patrol the sand, weaving amongst frisbee players, sunworshipers working on the famous California tan, volleyball games, children frolicking in the waves and building sand castles, and groups of junior lifeguards learning everything they

need to know from swimming in the ocean to cardio-pulmonary resuscitation. These junior lifeguards will one day be the lifeguards patrolling the beaches and protecting the fifty-nine million people a year who come to the beach to have fun in the warm California sun.

The water is full of swimmers, boogie boarders and, where surfing is permitted, surfers dot the waves. Farther out, beautiful sailboats glide effortlessly by with the wind in their sails, and windsurfers try to catch a wave, sometimes mastering the art and leaping over waves like soaring dolphins. Thus, the sand isn't the only place the lifeguards watch over. A team of lifeguards patrol offshore in Scarabs, the largest boats in the lifeguard fleet, or other rescue boats, looking to prevent accidents as well as watching for any existing trouble, whether it be surfers, sailboats, amateur windsurfers, or any other water-related emergencies.

These beachgoers come day after day to frolick and have the time of their lives at the beach. But a lifeguard's job, contrary to popular belief, is no beach boy's day at the beach. A common perception of the job "lifeguard" is that it is something you do until you get a "real job". But in fact, nothing could be more real than saving someone's life. For most lifeguards, the addiction of saving lives is what hooks them. Veteran lifeguard of twenty years and production consultant for Baywatch, Scott Hubbell, sums it up: "The ocean is the mother. To be this close to the mother, to study mankind from the windows of your lifeguard tower, and get paid to protect the people who come to enjoy it is a religious experience for me. It's a great feeling to know you can save someone's life." Simply stated, the job of the lifeguard is to assure that those who come to the beach to enjoy themselves go home alive.

The essence of lifeguarding is the camaraderie, the brotherhood, the fraternity of athletes who may also be lawyers, doctors or businessmen, coming together with a common goal – to protect people while they have fun. There are a lot of people walking around L.A. today who wouldn't be there if it weren't for the high quality of lifeguard standards. Lieutenant Tom Zahn is a legend, and he knows this to be true. At sixty years of age, he has spent his whole life as a lifeguard. He is personally responsible for more than 1,600 rescues, and never lost a person. For Zahn, the motivation for the type of person who becomes a lifeguard should be purity of heart. "It's a great feeling when you use what you've got and pull off a good one. There isn't any more rewarding and satisfying an occupation than lifesaving."

Lifeguarding, which has changed dramatically over the years, is practically a paramilitary organization that runs like a well-oiled machine. How else can you account for the fact that, in 1994, out of the almost sixty million visitors to L.A. county beaches, there were only three drownings?

Lifeguards save more lives than the police and fire departments combined. This is due to the training that the lifeguards are put through. The training methods and equipment of the L.A. county lifeguard system have become a model for representatives from all over the globe. Despite all of this, the old biases are hard to shake, and lifeguards consistently report that the public still, for the most part, sees them as playboys and beach bums . . . until one of them saves the life of a loved one. Then they are seen for what they really are – heroes.

There have been charges that the L.A. county's selection of lifeguards is unfair because it depends solely on swimming ability, ignoring other qualities such as judgment and the ability to deal with people. But L.A. County Lifeguard Association president, Ira Gruber, defends the importance of swimming. "I don't care how observant or cooperative they are . . . if they can't swim to that rescue on time, the rest doesn't matter." And so it begins with swimming. If you complete the ocean swim out around a buoy and back with sometimes hundreds of entrants and finish in the top fifty, you have made it to rookie school. Ten people are usually eliminated or drop out during rookie school, which has been described by many lifeguards as being tantamount to a hellish boot camp. First and foremost, rookie school stresses physical conditioning. Running and swimming miles per day is only the beginning of the grueling program. It literally separates the men from the boys . . . and the women from the girls.

Women weren't allowed to become lifeguards until 1972. That year, there were eight women lifeguards. There are only thiry-eight women lifeguards on the L.A. county roster now. Women must compete right alongside the men, with no special races, scorings or treatment. Beautiful, blonde twenty-four-year-old Diane Graner entered the lifeguard competition in 1982 and in the 1,000-meter open swim she beat all the men. There were no favors extended to her. She won on her own ability.

The image of an ocean lifeguard is usually one of a highly skilled athlete pulling people out of the water. While this is a vital part of the lifeguarding job, it is not the only one. In addition to rescue techniques, which include the correct procedure for everything from CPR (cardio-pulmonary resuscitation) to jellyfish attacks, prevention techniques are also an important part of the training program. A lifeguard does not sit back and wait for a rescue situation to arise. A good lifeguard is always scanning for potentially

hazardous situations and finding ways to prevent them. The concept behind prevention is simple: it is easier to stop a hazardous situation from developing than to deal with it after it develops. Any rescue that can be prevented eliminates potential injury to the victim as well as the lifeguard. Preventions include such actions as moving people away from rip currents – dangerous ocean currents that are the cause of eighty per cent of all ocean rescues; preventing the use of alcohol and drugs on the beach, especially preventing people under the influence from entering the water; removing unsafe flotation equipment from the water; waving off boats that are too close to the shore; keeping swimmers away from rock jetties and piers; and preventing people from entering the water in their clothes. While it might seem impressive for a lifeguard to have had fifty rescues in one day, a better record would be forty-eight prevents, two rescues.

Lifeguards are taught how to scan for other potential problems so that preventions can be made. The soft, untanned bodies that show up on the beach tip a lifeguard off to the fact that these people are unfamiliar with the sand and surf. "One of the cardinal rules of lifeguarding is, when in doubt, go out. Lifeguards don't wait for a victim to yell for help. Most are too panicked or embarrassed to yell out. Panicked looks and arms flailing about are all we need, and sometimes we don't even need that much," says Scott Hubbell.

Other areas of training include the use of lifesaving equipment, the operation of vehicles, techniques for pulling out floundering victims who want to crawl on top of your head, strenuous swim tests and a written exam. In addition to the rookies who are trained each year, all veteran lifeguards must undergo a lifeguard recheck. Basically, this consists of passing again everything you had to pass in rookie school to become a fully-fledged lifeguard. After all of this hard work, it is easy to see why lifeguards resent the beach-boy tag.

Stephanie Holden

Alexandra PAUL

Alexandra Paul on Stephanie Holden: "Her professional life is in order, but Stephanie's personal life is in disarray. The only person she could imagine growing old with is Mitch. Mitch is Stephanie's soulmate. If she could manage to go against character and lose control, she would lose it with Mitch. But she is afraid to lighten up for fear that no one else will be there to hold the fort. And this is very important to Stephanie.

There was a time in her early career when Stephanie was preoccupied with her husband at the time, and she missed a rescue which could have been fatal, if another hadn't intervened. No one knows this, not even Mitch. But this was the beginning of Stephanie's rigid, by-the-book attitude. It is hard for Stephanie to admit she has faults. When her sister Caroline missed a rescue because she was preoccupied with Logan, she should have shared this experience with Caroline. But Stephanie is afraid of appearing less than perfect, especially in Caroline's eyes."

Since Captain Thorpe's promotion and move downtown, Mitch has been standing in as supervising lieutenant at Baywatch but is looking forward to getting back to his tower once the new supervising lieutenant arrives. When beautiful, leggy, professional Stephanie Holden appears dressed in lifeguard uniform, Mitch cannot believe his eyes. Following his divorce, Mitch had a torrid love affair that was shattered when he was jilted by the woman. That woman was Stephanie Holden . . . Lieutenant Stephanie Holden, the woman with whom Mitch must now work professionally.

Mitch and Stephanie's relationship is strained until they both realize they must talk about what happened. They fell in love when Stephanie came to Baywatch as a temporary replacement and caught Mitch's eye. But Stephanie stood Mitch up when they were about to leave on a romantic getaway to Catalina. Since her temporary assignment at Baywatch was up, Stephanie left and Mitch never heard from her again. It is hard for Stephanie to admit, but she lied to Mitch: at the time of their affair, she was married.

She explains that she was actually separated and was getting a divorce, but the night before they were to go to Catalina, her husband begged for another chance. She decided to give their marriage one last try. She and her husband moved away, although even the change of scene wasn't enough to save their troubled marriage. They finally divorced, but Stephanie was sure Mitch would be so furious with her that he'd never speak to her again and so she never got in touch. That was two years ago, and since time heals all wounds, she hopes Mitch will forgive her. Of course he does, and he and Stephanie eventually become the best of friends.

Stephanie is by Mitch's side when he breaks his back and may never walk again. And when Stephanie is shot on a cruise ship and falls overboard, Mitch sees her fall and jumps after her to save her life. They are left adrift in the sea together, Stephanie bleeding and attracting sharks, as

the cruise ship sails off into the night, unaware of their plight. There is always an undercurrent of romantic feelings, particularly when Stephanie and Mitch go undercover as wealthy southern honeymooners in order to capture a group of modern-day pirates, and become attracted to the other's assumed character.

Ambitious in all she undertakes, Stephanie aspires to be the first female captain in the lifeguard service. She definitely has the qualifications: she is one hell of a lifeguard, a superior athlete, well educated and more feared and respected than she is liked. Matt Brody can certainly attest to the latter characteristic of this by-the-book, no-nonsense lady. When they meet in rookie school, Stephanie rides Matt so hard that he quits. But when he is persuaded to return and is eventually awarded the Rookie of the Year award, he gains something that means a great deal to him – Stephanie's respect.

When Stephanie meets new lifeguard and Olympic swimming hopeful, Cody Madison, she becomes his coach for the 1996 Olympics. Stephanie once had hopes of swimming in the Olympics herself, but an injury prevented her from competing. This is one of the major disappointments of her life.

Having CJ for a roommate proves to be a true test of nerves for Stephanie. CJ the sloppy and Stephanie the neat freak are always at each other. Stephanie can't stand to hear CJ's chanting, and CJ can't bear Stephanie's obsessive–compulsive nature. But, for better or for worse, they have each other and eventually grow to care a great deal for one another. When Caroline, Stephanie's sister, comes to town, she moves in with them, giving new meaning to the phrase "two's company . . . three's a crowd".

Since coming to Baywatch, Stephanie has had several love interests including Mark, a handsome Hawaiian lifeguard who teaches her, among other things, how to make rescues in huge Hawaiian surf on a wave runner. On a sailing trip to Catalina with CJ, Stephanie meets Roger, a sexy, rugged

coastguard officer. But her heart is stolen by Riley, a handsome ocean-ographer and environmentalist whom she meets when a severe earthquake hits L.A. After a romantic courtship, Riley begs Stephanie to set sail with him on a trip around the world on his yacht. No one, including Mitch, thinks that practical Stephanie will do such a thing, she is too responsible. But Stephanie surprises them all, and leaves for six weeks on the romantic adventure of a lifetime with her love, Riley.

When Stephanie returns she has to face one of the risks of being a lifeguard and spending so much time outdoors in the sun – skin cancer. With Mitch's support, Stephanie faces the possibility that she may have a melanoma. She is forced to evaluate where her life is at this point, and she realizes that if she survives, she would like to have children. But who would she like the father to be?

CJ Parker

Pamela ANDERSON

Pamela Anderson on CJ Parker:
"CJ lives in her own world, and sometimes it's hard for her to draw the line between reality and fantasy. But whatever world she's in, she loves life, and doesn't let things get her down.

She loves being a lifeguard, and puts her heart and soul into her job. There couldn't be anything more rewarding for CJ than saving people's lives, but saving animals is a real close second. Before CJ came to Baywatch, she was arrested for picketing to save the harp seals in Alaska. She wasn't arrested for picketing, she was arrested for picketing naked. she was making a statement. CJ would go through life naked before she would wear animal skin or fur of any kind. The person who understands CJ the best is Mitch. He understands her kookiness and her madcap ideas, and loves her all the more for them. Mitch was willing to let CJ keep an injured pelican that she'd rescued in his office, and even allowed her to put a mother cat who had just had a litter of kittens in his desk drawer. But when she asked him to keep a rescued seal in his bathtub, he said . . . "No, use your own."

While river rafting with fellow lifeguards and his son Hobie, Mitch discovers their river guide is none other than blonde, sexy, saxophone-playing Casey Jean Parker. CJ was a lifeguard at Baywatch years before, but she gave it all up to move to the river with the man of her dreams and become a river guide. She loves the river, but unfortunately the man of her dreams becomes the man of her nightmares. CJ has always gambled on men ... and lost. Growing up in Las Vegas, her father worked in a hotel casino and gambled away his salary. Her mother was a beautiful Las Vegas showgirl who loved CJ's father for all his faults, always forgiving him for losing all their money.

Mitch convinces CJ to come back to L.A. and Baywatch. She's afraid she won't pass the lifeguard recheck, but with Mitch's support she aces it and joins the Baywatch lifeguarding family. Settling into her new life, CJ rents an apartment only to find that it has been rented to another person at the same time – Baywatch's Lieutenant Stephanie Holden. CJ refuses to leave, and so does Stephanie. The two girls become reluctant roommates, driving each other crazy with their odd-couple antics.

Rather than being practical and logical like Stephanie, free-spirited, whimsical CJ, who prefers yoga

to working out, would just as soon read tea leaves or feel auras in order to make a decision. Alas, many of her decisions send her running to Mitch, her friend and confidant. Mitch was there for CJ when she needed a partner for a dance contest, when she thought a priest had fallen in love with her, when a devastating earthquake hit ... and when Cort left her.

For all their differences, Stephanie and CJ become close friends. When Stephanie's sister Caroline comes to town, she is welcomed into the fold ... and the apartment. For a while, CJ and Caroline are both attracted to Matt, but CJ wins his heart, and the two begin a serious relationship. While on a cruise, Matt is surprised to learn that CJ is a blackjack expert. He soon realizes CJ has a gambling addiction, and confronts her with her problem. CJ explains to Matt what it was like growing up in Las Vegas, and how she was bitten by the gambling bug. Matt helps CJ gain control of her addiction, and their relationship deepens.

CJ's expertise is helping others – both animals and humans. Some of CJ's happiest moments are spent in San Diego working with dolphins,

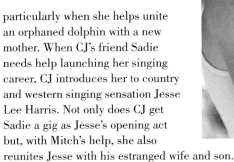

particularly when she helps unite an orphaned dolphin with a new mother. When CJ's friend Sadie needs help launching her singing career, CJ introduces her to country and western singing sensation Jesse Lee Harris. Not only does CJ get Sadie a gig as Jesse's opening act but, with Mitch's help, she also reunites Jesse with his estranged wife and son.

Just when Matt and CJ are spending more and more time together and find they are falling in love, Cort comes back into CJ's life. She is forced to face her true feelings and make a decision between the two men. Matt is now in love with CJ, but Cort wants her back. Matt is extremely jealous of CJ's need to help Cort and his struggle with his diminishing eyesight, but his fears are soon calmed. CJ chooses Matt. Her commitment to him is complete and when they have an opportunity to go to Hawaii together, they have a

wonderfully romantic holiday touring the island and hiking to a waterfall where they swim in a secluded lagoon surrounded by nothing but lush green jungle.

For CJ Christmas is children, so during the festive season she heads a group of orphaned children and gives them a special Christmas to remember, including decorating trees ... and lifeguard towers. But her uproariously fun time comes when Matt confides in her that he thinks Santa's elves are visiting his beach and leaving him presents in his tower.

When Matt saves the life of a beautiful Dutch tourist, Greta, who thinks she must serve Matt forever since she owes him her life, CJ concocts a plan to have Greta save Matt's life so that they will be even. Only then would overbearing Greta, and her eel lunches, be out of their lives forever. But CJ soon realizes her plan will never work. When Greta really does save Matt's life, CJ thinks it is one of her clever schemes, not realizing Greta actually saved him!

CJ isn't only there for her man during the good times. When Matt is suspended from Baywatch on charges of sexually harassing Neely Capshaw, a female lifeguard, CJ stands by him, knowing the charges are bogus. CJ entraps Neely into admitting on tape that she made the whole story up, but the tape is deemed inadmissible evidence in court. Neely is reinstated as a lifeguard at Baywatch, and Matt, unable to take the unfair decision, returns to France.

CJ follows Matt to France, but upon her return without him, CJ finds Mitch's shoulder a great one to lean on. And when she shares an important secret with him, their friendship develops into something more. CJ and Mitch realize they have romantic feelings for one another and it isn't long before they find themselves in each other's arms.

Caroline Holden

Yasmine BLEETH

After divorcing her environmentalist husband for being unfaithful to her, Stephanie's younger sister Caroline leaves her home in northern California and arrives at Stephanie and CJ's apartment unannounced and needing a place to stay. She has come to L.A. to start a new life and she wants to be a lifeguard. Stephanie trained Caroline for years on her strength swimming, and she is willing to train hard for rookie school. Caroline knows it will be a lot of hard work, but she wants to make the commitment to lifeguarding and saving lives. What she doesn't bargain for is the massive earthquake that hits L.A. on her first night, scaring the wits out of her and trapping Stephanie in a life-or-death situation.

After he rescues her sister, Caroline is instantly attracted to tall, dark and handsome lifeguard Matt Brody. But it isn't long before she is also attracted to cocky, arrogant, sexy lifeguard Logan Fowler. While she and Logan train for rookie school, Caroline confides in him that she doubts her ability. Logan tells Caroline that she won't have any trouble making it because her sister is in charge. Caroline wants to make it on her own, and assures Logan that there will be no favoritism. Besides, no matter how much her sister may favor her, only the first people to cross the line after the swim are in, and there is nothing Stephanie can do if she isn't one of the first. Caroline is

thrilled beyond belief when she does qualify for rookie school.

Stephanie does not like Logan, and thinks the world of Matt, so when Caroline tells Stephanie that she is not going to see Matt any more and concentrate on Logan, Stephanie is furious with her. Caroline just wishes Stephanie could see her and treat her like an adult, not a child. And who is she anyway to think she can pick the best guy for her? She couldn't pick the best guy for herself – otherwise she would have chosen Mitch instead of her loser of an ex-husband. But when Caroline finds out that Logan is seeing Kathleen – an older, rich and beautiful woman – behind her back, she just knows she will be unable to work the same beach with him.

When Caroline graduates from rookie school, she does end up on the same beach as Logan and, as she predicted, disaster hits. Caroline misses a rescue because she has her eyes on Logan while he talks to some beautiful girls on the beach. Caroline apologizes to Stephanie, telling her she was right about Logan in the first place. But charming Logan manages to convince Caroline that he cares about her, worming his way back into her arms.

Once she gets a handle on her emotions and puts her love life in perspective, Caroline excels and becomes a very skilled and competent lifeguard. In her rookie year, Caroline has to deal with a man who insists his daughter went down in the water off Caroline's tower. Caroline searches

exhaustively, but no body is found. Caroline takes this very hard until she finds out the man is reliving the trauma of his daughter's drowning ... a year ago.

With Mitch's help, Caroline rescues a beautiful Chinese refugee who is suffering from exposure adrift at sea on a makeshift raft. She helps the woman get her life together and find a home in America. When left in charge of headquarters, Logan and Caroline have their hands full keeping two reckless kids on wave runners from hurting themselves and others.

After rescuing a man suffering from AIDS, Caroline befriends him and helps him face up to living with this virus. Caroline makes a similar kind of rescue when she meets blind jockey Corey Barrons. Corey, the nation's leading jockey, lost his eyesight in a terrible accident on the racetrack. Caroline discovers that he has regained his eyesight but is still pretending to be blind because he is afraid to get back on a horse and ride. They strike up a friendship and Caroline helps Corey face his fear and ride again.

While in Hawaii, Caroline lives the moment she has dreamed of when Logan proposes to her. Then she lives the moment any woman would dread when she finds Logan is cheating on her, and gives him back his ring. Fortunately, the new lifeguard in town, Cody Madison, is very nearby when Caroline needs a handsome shoulder to cry on.

ART IMITATES LIFE

Baywatch heroes

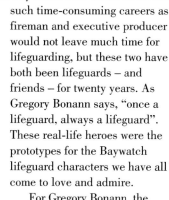

Michael Newman and Gregory Bonann are both L.A. county lifeguards, and both work on Baywatch. Michael Newman is an actor and a fireman. Gregory Bonann is one of the four creators and executive producers of Baywatch. One would think that such time-consuming careers as fireman and executive producer would not leave much time for lifeguarding, but these two have both been lifeguards – and friends – for twenty years. As Gregory Bonann says, "once a lifeguard, always a lifeguard". These real-life heroes were the prototypes for the Baywatch lifeguard characters we have all come to love and admire.

For Gregory Bonann, the line between life and art is often an extremely fine one. Bonann, in his capacity as executive producer, took several new Baywatch scriptwriters down to Venice beach for a tour, to familiarize them with what goes on in the world of lifeguarding. The writers received a first-hand

demonstration of a lifeguard's duty when Bonann, off duty at the time, was called upon to make a life-or-death ocean rescue.

A boy ran up to Bonann crying out that his brother had been swept out to sea and was drowning. Even though fully clothed, Bonann wasted no time as he ran toward the surfline, stripping off his clothes on the way. He could see the muddied water of a riptide current, but no victim in sight as he hit the water. After three dives in a systematic search pattern, Bonann spotted the boy, approximately eight feet underwater. There was no time to wait to get the boy to shore to administer CPR. With no rescue can for flotation, and while treading water some 120 yards offshore, Bonann performed mouth-to-mouth resuscitation on the unconscious boy. The boy responded by breathing, but before Bonann could get him to shore, three-foot waves crashed over them, submerging them both, and the boy stopped breathing again.

Bonann made his way toward the shore administering mouth-to-mouth resuscitation while waves continued to crash over him and the boy. On getting the boy to shore, backup had arrived, pure oxygen was administered and the boy was then taken to the hospital by paramedics. "In a rescue situation, the lifeguard separates himself from the emotion of the scene," says Bonann.

Even though the boy was submerged under water for seven minutes, he recovered completely. For saving that thirteen-year-old boy's life, Bonann was awarded the Medal of Valor, an annual award given for heroic acts, judged by fellow lifeguards. Bonann has his own thoughts on the award. "The Medal of Valor award goes to one person, but it really is a symbol of all the lifeguards out there who have made a difference in someone's life."

Michael Newman, who starred in the fifteen-minute presentation reel used to sell the series concept of Baywatch to NBC, has held four national titles for lifeguarding competitions. His most recent national title is for the Ironman competition – a combination of swimming, paddleboard and dory races – a victory won over many lifeguards some ten and twenty years his junior. So what's it like to be a fireman, lifeguard and actor all rolled into one? "Being a lifeguard and a firefighter is what I pretend to be when I'm working on Baywatch. Firefighting and

BAYWATCH

lifeguarding are very similar. Both are rescue work. I have a tower at the beach for lifeguarding, and the fire station where I work is at the beach, so in essence I have a tower there also. Both lifeguarding and firefighting are action-packed, beach emergencies in fire-ridden, flood-ravaged Malibu. Then when I go to work as an actor on Baywatch, I can recreate everything I do in real life!" Newman, who portrays himself on Baywatch, played a lifeguard and a fireman in one of the most recent Baywatch episodes. He was actually able to incorporate all three of his careers into one memorable, action-packed Baywatch episode, aptly titled "Hot Stuff".

What has been Newman's most frightening experience as a lifeguard? "I would have to say my first day of lifeguarding my rookie year. I was alone in my tower, no other guards within a half mile to the north or south ... and I knew that everyone on that crowded summer beach was relying on me, entrusting their lives to me. The enormity of the responsibility hit me as I sat there alone. No amount of working out with the seasoned guards or hearing stories about lifeguarding from them really prepared me for that feeling. It was terrifying."

Michael Newman is a big, strapping, strong man. But one of his greatest assets as a lifeguard and a fireman is his gentleness. He's not a big, tough guy when he's helping people. He sees people at their lowest points, when they don't always need muscle as much as they need gentleness and caring. It is important, when dealing with families of victims, to comfort them. "He's gonna be alright ... this is what we do ... he's got the best care imaginable right now," says Newman. This is what people need to hear. There are victims other than the ones injured, and they need emotional help.

Logan Fowler

Jaason **SIMMONS**

Jaason Simmons on Logan Fowler:
"For Logan, the ultimate way to get someone is to get them involved with you emotionally. Logan would like to sleep with Stephanie Holden to gain power over her and be able to manipulate her. If Logan could just get inside her mind and mess with her, he could push her out of Baywatch. It would be fun to play Caroline against Stephanie. Logan would like to show people, especially Caroline, that Stephanie isn't as strong and together as she seems, and that Logan would be better in her position as lieutenant. And next, maybe take over Mitch's job... who knows."

Hunky, sassy Australian Logan Fowler comes to Baywatch just as a massive earthquake rocks California. Logan is a seasoned lifeguard who transfers over from Australia. He has a bit of a chip on his shoulder because he resents having to go through rookie school, when he has been a guard for many years in Australia. But Mitch explains to him that if you want to be a lifeguard on L.A. county beaches, you have to attend their rookie school. During the earthquake, Logan proves his worth as a lifeguard.

Stephanie wishes Logan wasn't such a good lifeguard because it would make it so much easier for her to dislike him. And Stephanie doesn't like or trust him, especially when he sets his sights on her sister, Caroline. When Logan gets into an argument with Matt over Caroline, and Matt accuses Logan of being careless during a rescue, Logan accuses Matt of being jealous. A fight ensues, and Stephanie decides the two of them need extended time together to learn how to work with each other. She

puts them in a dory out on the ocean and makes them row back to shore together. They end up having to rescue two drowning boys, and do so with teamwork. But Stephanie is still not convinced that Logan should be at Baywatch.

When Caroline misses a rescue because her eyes are on Logan, Stephanie reassigns him to another beach. He threatens to sue for sex discrimination, and Caroline is furious with her sister for butting in. When Mitch tells Stephanie that Logan has a case, she has no choice but to apologize and reassign him to Baywatch.

Logan sets his sights on Kathleen Huntington, an older, beautiful, wealthy Malibu widow. After she snubs him at the beach club, Logan pays a guy to attack her so he can become her hero by rescuing her. His plan works like a charm, and Kathleen falls head over heels for her hero. Logan would like to have Caroline, but what he

really needs is a green card in order to stay in the States. He gets his green card by marrying Kathleen, and breaking Caroline's heart.

Eventually, Logan ends his marriage to Kathleen and Caroline takes him back. But he is soon back to his conniving, manipulative ways again.

Cody Madison comes to town and immediately rubs Logan the wrong way because Logan senses Caroline is attracted to Cody. As a result, Logan does everything he can to undermine Cody as a lifeguard. The only person who is really on to Logan is Neely Capshaw. They are a great deal alike, and Neely has his number.

While in Hawaii, Logan, who is chosen to pose for publicity pictures with the Hawaiian Tropic girls, finds himself in hot water with Caroline until he proposes to her with orchids spelling out "Will You Marry Me?" in the sand. Caroline accepts his proposal, but it is not long before Logan louses things up and she gives him back his ring.

Neely Capshaw

Gena Lee NOLIN

Gena Lee Nolin on Neely Capshaw: "Neely is a very insecure girl. She's a good person, but she does bad things. What she really wants is acceptance and love, but goes about it in the only way she knows how to get what she wants . . . by using her looks. Neely has always gotten what she wants based on her looks. She had to in order to survive having six older brothers who took every minute of her father's time. The only way she could get his attention was by looking pretty and using her feminine wiles. And it worked, and that's how Neely tries to make her entire life work. She really just wants to be loved and nurtured, poor thing."

Beautiful, blonde vixen Neely Capshaw is transferred to Baywatch and immediately hits on Matt when they share a tower together. She makes a pass at him, but Matt tells her he has a girlfriend and isn't interested. When Neely is late to a rescue and Matt smells liquor on her breath during CPR, he confronts Neely about drinking on the job. She begs him not to turn her in, but Matt knows he has to – she could endanger her life, and the lives of others, by being intoxicated on the job.

When Mitch and Matt confront Neely, she flies into a rage, claiming that Matt came on to her in the tower and wouldn't take no for an answer. Now she claims his male ego is hurt and he has made up this story to get even. CJ eventually entraps Neely with her lie, but Matt has already been suspended. It is Neely's word against Matt's, and she is reinstated at Baywatch.

Mitch is keeping his eye on Neely. Stephanie and Caroline don't trust her, and CJ gets into a cat fight with her and almost scratches her eyes out. Cody, who doesn't know anything about her, saves her life while they are both trapped underwater during a rescue, and Neely reciprocates by saving his. Thus, her only friendship at Baywatch is formed.

Neely is a girl with a plan to get ahead. Her power lies in finding everyone's Achilles heel and storing the information for her future use. But even with her abundance of character flaws, Neely is a good lifeguard – and hopefully isn't drinking on the job any longer.

Cody Madison

David CHOKACHI

Stephanie first lays eyes on Cody Madison when he is swimming at the pool where she coaches a girls' swim team. The girls can't take their eyes off this stunning blond Adonis. Stephanie can't take her eyes off his beautiful and powerful freestyle swimming stroke. She is surprised when the coach at the pool tells her that Cody didn't make the Olympic cut. It wasn't ability he lacked, he just didn't have the motivation.

Stephanie learns that Cody recently lost both of his parents when they drowned in a flood back east. She sympathizes and realizes why he has lost his fight to win. Much to Caroline's dismay, Stephanie takes Cody under her wing, gets him a lifeguarding job at Baywatch and becomes his coach for the 1996 Olympics in Atlanta.

When an oil-rig platform collapses in the ocean, Cody saves fellow newcomer Neely Capshaw's life while they work to save others trapped below the ocean surface. And Neely reciprocates by saving Cody, forming an instant bond between the two of them. Being new at Baywatch, Cody is not aware of Neely's bogus harassment suit against Matt, and becomes her only friend.

At first Cody thinks he still lacks the motivation to make it to the Olympics. But when Logan eggs him on, calling him a quitter, Cody realizes he does want to win, and he is willing to train hard. Stephanie is thrilled, and when they take off on a Catalina endurance swim, Cody has to make the decision to free dive to save a young girl whose boat flips over. Stephanie wants to make the dive, fearing he could injure his lungs or ears. But Cody dives before she can stop him. When he comes back to headquarters a hero – much to Logan's dismay – Stephanie and Caroline hover over him like mother hens, bringing him ice packs and praise.

There is no doubt about it, Cody Madison is on his way to the Olympics. He is going for gold.

So many beaches, so little time

The beach, the beach, the beach. Except for one day a week on stage, the Baywatch cast and crew can be found filming on any one of the many beaches along the southern California coast. Several beaches are used for filming, all having something different to offer the beachgoer. How does one decide on which beach one will spread a towel, prop an umbrella, slather on the suntan lotion, dip in the cool surf, and enjoy a day at the beach?

First, there's Venice State beach, world famous for its funky, artistic atmosphere, circus-like entertainers, roller-bladers, colorful characters and wild music. Venice was among the first beaches to offer lifeguard protection in the 1920s and there are now twenty lifeguard towers along this stretch of beach. Venice is probably the most cosmopolitan beach area in the county of Los Angeles. Its population of writers, artists, filmmakers, elderly retired people, youth gangs, surfers, roller-bladers, and homeless people make it a blend of the very rich and the very poor living and playing together. Tourists flock to Venice beach, attracted by the bike path, the shopping, and the great beach with its many activities.

Moving further north to the Santa Monica State beach area, the beaches are terrific for swimming, body surfing and boogie boarding. The landmark Santa Monica pier, one of the most famous sights in Los Angeles, is located along this stretch of beach. The pier is often used as a location for Baywatch, whether it be for its gaiety and carnival-type atmosphere, including a merry-go-round, a ferris wheel and many arcades and shops, or for the labyrinth of beams supporting the pier underneath, creating a moody atmosphere. Unfortunately, the pier also attracts thrill seekers who wish to jump off the end. This is illegal and dangerous, and yet another situation for the lifeguards to monitor.

The bike path continues through this beach and on up the coast to Will Rogers State beach, named after Will Rogers, the famous American humorist known as the "cowboy philosopher". Jogging, fishing, scuba and skin diving, surfing and beach volleyball are all popular activities at this beach. If you follow the bike path along this stretch of beach you will pass by Will Rogers Headquarters, the headquarters used in Baywatch. In addition to the headquarters building, some twenty-four lifeguard towers dot the sand. This beach area is made up of stretches of sand with rock jetties protruding out into the water. The jetties, built to help prevent sand erosion, are a major draw to those who like to rock climb. But this can prove

dangerous, and lifeguards must watch carefully as no signs are posted on the jetties, warning people of the danger. One of the problems with many of the popular beaches is parking. It is very limited. Will Rogers is particularly popular because of its versatile activities and its huge parking lot which accommodates almost 2,000 cars.

Further north is Malibu Surfrider beach, always dotted with surfers waiting for the perfect wave. It is renowned as a particularly excellent surfing area. It also has a calm area of water to the south for bathers, and a lagoon. But surfing is the main draw. The name Malibu is said to be a derivative of the Chumash Indian word "humaliwo", which means "where the surf sounds loudly". There are only three lifeguard towers on this beach and it is important for lifeguards to keep swimmers and boogie boarders clear of the surfing areas in order to prevent collisions. Surfrider beach is bordered on the south by the Malibu pier, great for fishing and boat excursions, and on the north by the Malibu Colony, lined with multi-million-dollar homes where the movie stars live and play. Malibu is extremely popular among tourists who flock to see this beach, made famous in the surfing movies of the 50s and 60s, with the hopes of perhaps catching a glimpse of a movie star or two.

When Baywatch cannot go on location to such places as Hawaii, the American River in California, San Diego, or a cruise ship – as they have in the past – but want to depict an exotic place, they move further north to Zuma beach and Leo Carillo beach. The remote settings, rocky caves and treacherous cliff faces found at these beaches often serve as other locales such as Catalina or Mexico. People from all over the world come to these beaches to see where Baywatch is filmed. They are never let down. Even though there is security, there are ample opportunities to watch the filming, and even some chances for autographs from their favorite Baywatch characters.

Matt Brody

David CHARVET

Tall, dark, handsome, high school student Matt Brody roars into town on his motorcycle with a chip on his shoulder. His family recently moved to L.A. from France, and his wealthy father wavers between emotional neglect of Matt and control over him. Matt's father doesn't think lifeguarding is an appropriate career for such an irresponsible guy, a guy who never finishes what he starts. Tired of always being put down by his father, rebel Matt decides he has found his vocation in lifeguarding.

He has an opportunity to prove to his father, and to himself, that he can cut it. An excellent swimmer and member of the high school swim team, Matt decides to enter the rookie qualifying swim. Matt's swimming ability gets him into lifeguard rookie school, where he then comes nose to nose with Lieutenant Stephanie Holden. She informs everyone that this is the "boot camp" of lifeguarding, and she takes an instant dislike to tardy, disruptive, sassy Matt, who she feels is not taking lifeguarding seriously. Between his father's criticisms and Stephanie's riding him, Matt quits rookie school. Mitch, who sympathizes with Matt's troubled father–son relationship, convinces him to return.

Before long, Matt has a chance to prove to Stephanie just how seriously he does take lifeguarding, and Mitch and Stephanie award him the Rookie of the Year award. This award is bestowed upon the rookie who, after placing in the top twelve, distinguishes himself in some way. Matt risked not

placing at all by stopping to help Summer during the final race, and received the award for teamwork, which is what lifeguarding is all about.

Matt soon finds himself in love with Summer Quinn. When he has recurring nightmares of being attacked by a shark, Summer interprets his dreams for him. He doesn't have a fear of sharks, he has a fear of commitment. Namely, commitment to her. Summer decides to leave town, and attend college back east.

Matt is surprised, but not sad, to hear that his father is moving back to France. When he says goodbye to his father, not wishing to return to France with him, his father takes Matt's motorcycle away and cuts him off without a dime. With no place to live, Stephanie suggests that Matt moves in with her and CJ. When CJ finds out about Stephanie's generous offer, she is aghast. Doesn't Stephanie know that she is attracted to Matt and has zero willpower to resist him? Stephanie tells her to get a grip, and Matt moves in. Matt is also attracted to CJ, and they fight it for a while, until it is useless. Matt and CJ get involved and fall in love.

Over the years, Matt has been responsible for quite a few miraculous rescues. He saved Summer from a twenty-foot octopus and, on another occasion, from a great white shark ready to devour her. When Matt and Jimmy Slade bungee jump from a hot-air balloon as part of their competition for Summer, Matt heroically cuts his own bungee cord and jumps to save Jimmy who is hanging upside down, submerged underwater.

But when lifeguard Neely Capshaw accuses Matt of sexually harassing her, no one can save him from suspension – not even CJ, who gets Neely to admit that the charges against Matt are bogus. As much as he loves CJ and lifeguarding, Matt cannot bear to continue under the circumstances and returns home to France.

Alexandra Paul (Stephanie Holden) on Matt Brody: "When Matt Brody first came to Baywatch, he had a lot of anger, mostly directed toward his father and the lack of family life that he craved while he was growing up. He was able to find a role model and father figure in Mitch, and a family with the lifeguards at Baywatch. Stephanie was particularly tough on him because she thought his hormones got the better of him, and knew he had the potential to be a terrific lifeguard. Stephanie really developed a deep fondness for Matt, and wished he hadn't fled to France after Neely accused him of sexual harassment. He wasn't guilty, and she wishes he'd stayed and faced her. He's lucky to have CJ in his life, she really grounds him, and is good for him. Stephanie thought Matt would be great for her sister Caroline, but she loves CJ as a sister too, and Caroline will just have to find someone else big sister approves of. Maybe Cody Madison ... unless, of course, Stephanie decides to keep him for herself."

Summer Quinn

Nicole EGGERT

Summer and her mother Jackie drive their trailer cross country to pursue Jackie's dream of becoming a singer – and to escape Jackie's abusive boyfriend. Summer enrolls in Malibu High and, being an excellent swimmer and needing a good job that pays well, she decides to sign up for the rookie school qualification swim to become a lifeguard.

Out of the hundreds who participate in this gruelling swim, only twenty-five will qualify for rookie school, and out of those, only twelve will claim a position as lifeguard. Summer is discouraged, but that doesn't keep her from doing her best. She does place and she does make it to rookie school. So does Matt Brody. Summer and Matt become friends when Matt rescues her and her mother from her mother's abusive boyfriend, who tries to push their trailer over a cliff – with them in it!

The ordeal to become a lifeguard has only just begun. Summer and Matt attend rookie school together. They have to make it through a written

exam, a physical, and a psychological profile. During this process, many rookies are weeded out, leaving the final test. The run–swim–run, and the forty-foot pier jump. Summer is scared to death to make this jump, and she freezes. Matt risks not finishing when he stays behind with her until she can jump. They make the jump together and swim like crazy for the finish. They both place, and make the final cut. Falling into each other's arms with joy, a bond is made and a lasting friendship formed.

Summer and her mother Jackie are very close. Jackie is supportive of Summer's lifeguarding career, but Summer is a little embarrassed by Jackie's career which often finds her singing in places that her friends' rich Malibu parents frequent. When Jackie gives up singing to take over the local lifeguard beach hut café, Summer is thrilled. When it looks like Jackie won't be ready for the grand opening in time, all the lifeguards pitch in and help Jackie get the café ready. Jackie and Summer proudly look on their new baby, Jackie's Summer Place. Her food soon becomes the hit of the beach, and everyone eventually ends up here for a meal or snack.

Summer finally lands the guy of her dreams, surfer Jimmy Slade. When Summer is held hostage in her tower by a madman, Jimmy tries to rescue her, but is shot in the shoulder and forced to retreat. He recovers, and soon after goes away for a while on a surfing circuit.

Finding himself falling for Summer, Matt realizes his friendship with Jimmy is strained. Can he move in on his friend's girl while he is out of town? Summer and Matt can't help what they feel for one another and start dating.

Summer is shocked when Jimmy appears in front of her tower unannounced. She didn't know he was coming back and she doesn't know what to say. When Jimmy hears about Matt and Summer, he and Matt decide to settle it their own way. After almost losing his life and being rescued by Matt, Jimmy leaves town permanently to pursue his surfing career, and Summer and Matt continue to build their relationship.

When Summer suffers from bulimia, Matt helps her through it. When she suddenly develops a fear of water, Matt helps her face the truth. She was locked in a jacuzzi by her stepfather when she was a child, and she had repressed the memory. When a ghost haunts their hotel room and falls in love with Summer, who resembles his lost love, Matt is the only one who can break the spell the ghost has over Summer. He rescues her when the ghost tries to lure Summer to her death so that she can join him forever.

Summer loves Matt very much, but feels that he is not ready to commit to her. She decides to go back east to attend college, leaving her mother, her lifeguarding career – and Matt – behind.

Jimmy Slade

Kelly SLATER

To say Jimmy Slade is just a surfer is an understatement. He is the best surfer on the west coast and left home at sixteen to pursue his dream of becoming the world surfing champion. He lives in his van with his surfboard and a few boxes of cereal. Summer Quinn develops an instant crush on this sexy blond guy.

While investigating reports of a surf gang attacking other surfers in the water, lifeguard Matt Brody meets fellow surfer Jimmy Slade. Striking up a friendship while they surf, they are attacked by the gang. This group of territorial surfers don't like other surfers in their water. Slashing other surfers' tires while they are catching waves, breaking into their cars or picking fights in the water is the way they operate. The gang makes their message clear to Matt and Jimmy, this is their water . . . stay out.

When Summer asks for surfing lessons, Jimmy can't turn her down. Taking the waves together is exhilarating, until they are attacked by the same surf gang. This time they have set a deadly trap for Jimmy – they have put barbed wire in the ocean! Jimmy is rescued and the gang is caught and

hauled away by the lifeguards. He may be new in town, but Jimmy already has a great friend in Matt, and a terrific girlfriend in Summer.

Just when he thought his life was perfect, Jimmy's father, a career marine, tracks him down. He insists that Jimmy returns home with him. Jimmy is sick of living on army bases and moving all the time. When Jimmy refuses to go with him, his father punches him, sending him to the ground. Jimmy remembers the other reason he doesn't want to go back with his father. He's tired of being a punching bag. Jimmy won't fight back, he just wants to surf. Disgusted with his son, his father leaves, but not before busting Jimmy's surfboard in half over his knee.

Jimmy is left alone by his father to pursue his dream. When he meets a rich, beautiful, snobby girl from Malibu Beach High who wants to be his personal manager and sponsor him in his surfing competitions, he jumps at the chance. Summer is less enthusiastic and more jealous, since she knows the girl, and knows exactly what the "personal" part of the managing will entail. Eventually, Jimmy leaves town and it isn't long before he realizes his dream. He becomes the number one surfer in the world at the age of eighteen.

The rules of the game

L.A. county lifeguard towers are manned during all daylight hours. In summer, that's some twelve hours of daylight to cover. Each lifeguard is responsible for approximately 300 to 400 yards of ocean. During the winter when the crowds are considerably less, and the number of working lifeguards falls from 600 to 108, there are fewer towers open. Thus, a single lifeguard may have to be responsible for up to one and a half miles of water. Winter brings different kinds of rescues, according to lifeguard of eighteen years and actor on Baywatch, Michael Newman. "The beaches may be less crowded, but it's not the time to kick back and read a book. During the winter a situation can become serious much quicker due to storm conditions, larger surf and colder water."

Lifeguards have rules – many rules – that must be strictly adhered to or the result could be a life lost. The cardinal rule is always to watch the water. A lifeguard's back is never to be turned to the water. Even when coming up his ramp, a lifeguard backs up, his eyes always fixed on the water.

When a lifeguard is watching his water, wearing his red trunks, he is the big man on campus. Everyone is watching him. The people on the beach

expect the lifeguard to watch over them – after all, that's his job. If a lifeguard is talking to anyone, he must keep his eyes on the water, not the person's face, and never allow anyone to obstruct his view. The twenty-second rule is unwritten, but often used: a lifeguard may not talk to any beachgoer for longer than twenty seconds, otherwise it is deemed unprofessional.

Several forms of communication are available to the lifeguards. Each lifeguard tower has a telephone connected to a switchboard in lifeguard headquarters, which also allows communication directly between lifeguard towers. This phone system is considered emergency equipment and is not meant for personal use. All lifeguard emergency vehicles and Baywatch rescue boats are equipped with departmental radios, allowing a wide range of communications ship-to-ship and ship-to-shore. These communications are essential to a lifeguard's job.

A lifeguard is never to be without his most important piece of equipment, the rescue can. Rescue cans are floats made of hard plastic with handles molded into the sides and rear. The can is attached to a line and harness which is worn by the lifeguard over one shoulder when making a rescue. This can was designed to support up to seven non-hysterical people in the water. When a lifeguard is in his tower, his rescue can hangs overhead. Any time the lifeguard leaves the tower, that rescue can must be in hand. When a lifeguard goes into the water to make a save, the first thing he will say to the victim is "take the can". The rescue can is the flotation device with which the lifeguard will safely bring in the victim. But Newman knows the kind of problems that can occur. "Trying to get two victims to take the can who are holding on to each other so tight that you can't pry them apart is a problem. They are terrified, think they are going to die, and are not in the real world any more. You must be able to get them to hold on to the rescue can for flotation." At this point, the lifeguard must keep the can between himself and the victim. The most important notion for a lifeguard to grasp is that he must stay alive to save a life. If the victim does not take the can but panics and climbs on top of the lifeguard, both of them are in serious jeopardy.

The most important rule about bringing a victim back to shore through the surf is never to lose contact with that victim. The lifeguard's plan is to make it back to shore during the lull, or calm, between "sets". A set is a series of waves that come in a rhythm. The swells, or waves, come in groupings of three to four waves at a time. When trying to get back to shore it is best to do so during a lull, but sometimes the rescue can't wait and a set of powerful waves is upon the lifeguard and victim. Newman has been there: "A victim can be slippery, especially when he's scared, and when you're thrown over the top of the waves, free falling fifteen feet sometimes holding on to the victim so he doesn't slip from your grasp, the force of the wave drives you to the bottom of the ocean. Sometimes you hit hard, and this is the moment of truth, because if you lose your grip on that victim, he won't make it."

A lifeguard must always survey his assigned area and prevent problems before they occur. The old saying, "an ounce of prevention is worth a pound of cure", couldn't be truer of the lifeguarding profession. Assessing the people on the beach and realizing who is a high risk goes a long way in making preventions. Children playing on the sand with rubber flotation toys are not far from taking them into the water and getting into trouble because the toys can easily be popped once in the surf. The lifeguard must explain to the children and their parents why the flotables are not safe. He then

needs to continue to keep an eye on the children to be sure they remember what he said later on in the day. Preventing disasters before they happen is the lifeguard's most valuable technique.

Backup is a crucial component of every rescue. The majority of rescues are completed by the lifeguard on duty, but when the going gets tough and people are being sucked out to sea by a rip current, every lifeguard available is called upon. Even the most routine rescue can quickly escalate into an emergency requiring more than one lifeguard. To this end, a system has been developed to ensure that lifeguards will have backup each time they enter the water on a rescue. When a lifeguard needs extra help, he will knock his telephone off the hook in his tower, which is the signal for backup, or he may hail a guard in the neighboring tower. It is also the responsibility of lifeguards in adjoining towers to recognize when another guard is in need of backup.

A good lifeguard knows his daily beach like a map. First of all, he has checked out the bottom of the ocean that he is responsible for. He knows the inshore holes, the water temperature and the surf conditions. He knows approximately who is on his beach and where they are. He knows if the mother of the children who are playing in the surf is sleeping. He knows that the people who are still wearing clothes probably can't swim, but may try to go into the water wearing their clothes. "A good lifeguard has the instincts of a shark. He can spot a weak swimmer and zero in on him," says Newman.

If surfers are not at a strictly surfing beach, swimmers and surfers cannot be in the water at the same time. A red flag posted at the lifeguard tower means bathers only, and a flag with a black ball on it means surfboards are banned. At beaches designated for surfers, surf conditions can be crowded, there is a great deal of competition, and surfing etiquette has to be observed. It is up to the lifeguard to recognize hazardous surfing situations, including territorial surf gangs in the water.

These surf gangs, which may have from three to eight members, decide that a certain area of water is theirs and no one else has the right to surf there. Of course, no one "owns" the waves, but these gangs think they do, and do their best – subtly or aggressively – to keep other surfers out of "their" territory and off "their" waves. These gangs may knock other surfers off their boards by cutting them up while surfing a wave. If this technique doesn't work, they might slash the unwanted surfer's car tires, or scratch his car. Often, surfers know they don't have to leave and are not intimidated by these gangs and their threats of damage to their possessions or bodily harm. Inevitably, fights break out between the surfers and the lifeguard on duty is the one who has to break up these fights. How do they break them up given that they have no weapons? "Well, being six feet five inches tall and 220

pounds helps," says Newman. But not all lifeguards have this stature, especially the women. Just one more difficult and often dangerous job for the lifeguards to take on wearing nothing more than a swimsuit.

L.A. county estimates that twenty-six million people went to southern California beaches in 1973. In the last twenty years, that number has more than doubled. As a result, problems at the beach have escalated over the years with the growing number of crowds, inner-city gangs hitting the beach, and the homeless and transient people living under lifeguard towers, piers, or anywhere else they can crash. Even though the city police departments have increased their patrols on the beach, it is not enough and lifeguards are being forced to act as police officers. However, lifeguards have only a citizen's power of arrest, and nothing more than their rescue can as a weapon to enforce the law or defend themselves against everything from gang fights to homicide. The areas of largest concern are the Santa Monica and Venice beaches, which are the most popular beaches for the homeless. In addition, the freeways that empty into these beach areas act as escapeways for inner-city gangs. Ideally, the police arrive on the scene of a volatile situation before the lifeguards need to get involved. But guards must occasionally deal with fights and situations involving guns and knives until the police take over the situation. The police, then, are like the backup for lifeguards, since the lifeguards are often the first on the scene simply because of their location. The crowds have changed over the years. People used to respect badges and authority. But now, police get little respect when they carry a gun and handcuffs – and a lifeguard certainly gets much less respect in a T-shirt and shorts.

And of course, what would a job be without paperwork? Each lifeguard keeps a log book in his tower to document his daily actions and observations. In addition, lifeguards must fill out an Ocean Rescue Report that accurately details every rescue he is involved in. Major rescues require an Incident Report to be filled out, and a First Aid Report for each time first aid is administered to a beachgoer.

Garner Ellerbee

Gregory ALAN-WILLIAMS

Gregory Alan-Williams on Garner Ellerbee:
"Garner is lonely, and misses being married. He has never admitted it, but he is still in love with his ex-wife. Mitch and Garner both lost their marriages because of their careers. They have never discussed this, and Garner would like to talk about these feelings with Mitch. Mitch dates, but Garner doesn't really want to date. He just wants to find true love. But this is difficult for a macho guy in this day and age to admit."

Born and raised in the east, Garner moves out west for a better, and warmer, life in sunny California. But he is a different kind of lifeguard. An inner-city lifeguard – a handsome, rugged black cop. Garner has never gotten over losing his partner during a routine traffic stop. When

he punches out his captain, Garner is demoted to a different beat: cop on beach patrol. Garner hates the sand and hates the water . . . but he hates his captain more. So, whether it's crime on the beach – a lost dog, breaking up a gang fight – or making arrests, Garner is there, patrolling the beach, the boardwalk, the pier, and beach communities on his four-wheel motorcycle.

Here he meets Mitch and the rest of the Baywatch guards. When the lifeguards are taken hostage in headquarters by escaped convicts, Garner, who has been shot and left for dead by the convicts, single-handedly saves his pals. While he becomes a part of their family, he never quite adjusts to sand in his socks.

Garner, whose attitude toward life is "keep on keepin' on", and whose idol is rodeo rider Bill Pickett, reveals to Mitch that his father was also a rodeo rider. Garner decides to try his beat on horseback. He loves the horse, but he doesn't love shoveling up what the horse leaves for him on top of the sand. His

horseback days don't last long, and Garner is soon back on his moped.

Mitch, who has become Garner's best friend, convinces him that the only way he is going to get off the beach beat is to apologize to his captain for punching him out. Garner says there is no way, but after a while longer on the beach, he decides to humble himself. After apologizing to his captain, Garner finds he is buried under paperwork in the cramped basement. Oh yes, his vengeful captain is getting even. It is not long before his captain antagonizes Garner to the point where he snaps. He punches out his captain again . . . and ends up back at the beach.

Garner loves to sing the blues, dress up as Santa at Christmas, play basketball, and does not want to hear his horoscope. He also has a fear of heights. When the only way to get help and save Mitch's life is for Garner to jump off a mountain hanging from a hang-glider, he runs screaming toward the cliff . . . but makes it to help and brings the lifeguards back to save Mitch.

When Garner suffers a mid-life crisis, it is Mitch who is there for him while he tries other careers. He eventually settles on the career he always wanted as a kid – private eye. Garner opens a detective agency and tries to convince Mitch to join him. He succeeds, and Mitch, becoming a lifeguard with a second career, joins Garner as his partner in the agency, along with another partner, Ryan McBride, who turns out to be a beautiful woman.

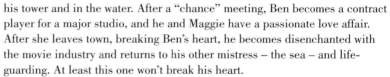

Ben Edwards lifeguarded on L.A. county beaches in the fifties when uniforms were trunks and tank tops, surfers would hang ten on long boards, and ocean pollution had never been heard of. During his rookie summer, Ben is discovered by a beautiful and famous actress, Maggie James, who lives on the beach and watches handsome, rugged, athletic Ben at work in his tower and in the water. After a "chance" meeting, Ben becomes a contract player for a major studio, and he and Maggie have a passionate love affair. After she leaves town, breaking Ben's heart, he becomes disenchanted with the movie industry and returns to his other mistress – the sea – and lifeguarding. At least this one won't break his heart.

Thirty years later, when the James mansion is being fixed up to sell, Ben, fearing Maggie must have died, investigates the old house. What he finds startles, mystifies and delights him. Maggie is alive . . . and living in the old mansion. They rekindle their romance, and reminisce about the old days.

Injured during a rescue, Ben is forced to use a cane to walk. This takes its toll on Ben, as it would any lifeguard. He is taken off the sand – which is tantamount to taking a fish out of water. Working in headquarters is difficult for Ben, and it is hard for Mitch to see him this way. Ben has always been like a father to Mitch, whose own father was less than thrilled with his career choice. When a nostalgic lifeguard reunion is planned for the Red Knights, an elite 1950s group of guards who have returned to relive their glory days, they are surprised to see Ben using a cane and confined to administrative duties.

Ben himself is not happy to be viewed in this light. Just when he is beginning to think his real lifeguarding days are over, Ben jumps fifty feet into the water, saving a small boy's life. He is still and always will be a lifeguard until the day he dies.

California gold

"There's nothing like swimming in a turquoise jewel and feeling your heart pump." Scott Hubbell, event promotor for over 200 beach events, competition director of the L.A. County Lifeguard Association, and production consultant for Baywatch, still cannot tear himself away from his true love . . . lifeguarding. In the 1920s, lifeguard meets started along the California beaches and still take place today. California guards compete mostly for pride – pride as athletes and pride as lifesavers.

The largest training ground in southern California for athletes is the beach. Hubbell throws big beach parties that have drawn over a million spectators and competitors over the last decade to the beaches. Most of these competitors are the southern California lifeguards, but there are a lot of people who are interested in the beach, ocean racing and other ocean events. These lifeguards are the real thing. They are simply the best ocean and water athletes. They are the top dogs and they dominate the events.

These competitions demonstrate that lifeguards are not just tan guys who hang out looking buffed. Lifeguards are competitive, and the events sharpen their skills as well as test them. The lifeguards' training for these events puts them in top physical shape to

protect the southern California beaches, as all events are rescue simulated. "I think these events epitomize the Californian lifestyle. It's the ocean lifestyle that people dream about elsewhere," says Hubbell.

Among the most exciting and dangerous events are the dory boat races. Dory boats, rowed by two lifeguards working as a team, were once used frequently in surf rescues, but more advanced rescue boats have since replaced them. These awkward, twenty-foot, self-baling boats are dangerous crafts, especially in large surf. Because of the extreme danger of capsizing, no one is allowed to race without a helmet.

California beach volleyball is also wildly popular and is open to the public so that anyone can participate. It is one of the fastest growing, most visible sports in California. Because of this, it has developed from being a game played on the beaches, to a sport that is played around the world. Volleyball at the southern California beach festivals is a great way to learn about the game without the intimidating atmosphere of the tournaments.

Of all the events, beach flags is considered to be the most fun. It is a test of agility and quickness that eliminates the slowest competitors. In each round there is one more competitor than flag – a modified piece of rubber hose. In a line, the competitors lie face down in the sand. At the starter's signal they rise, turn, and sprint to a flag, diving into the sand to grab it. The winner is the last person to have a flag, like musical chairs.

There are three specialty events that are combinations of individual events. The Ultra Waterman, which was created by Scott Hubbell, combines the 400-meter swim, a 600-meter paddleboard, a 600-meter surf ski, and a 600-meter dory. Completion time is about fifteen to twenty minutes. The International Ironman consists of the surf ski, paddleboard and swim events, also taking about fifteen to twenty minutes. Interestingly, in Australia, they

take anywhere from two to four hours to complete this event because they compete over longer distances. The American Ironman consists of the dory, paddleboard and swim events.

While these summer festivals bring together some of the world's finest ocean athletes in exciting competition, most events are open to the public. People who are into training at the beach are encouraged to come down and participate and also to watch the top athletes, usually the lifeguards, compete.

In order to excel in these events, one must have a good knowledge of the ocean. The competitors must be able to read the surf conditions and respect mother nature. It's not unusual to see someone who has fallen behind in a race use his water knowledge to pick up a wave with precise timing, pass another competitor and win. It's more than lifeguard against lifeguard; it's lifeguard against lifeguard against the ocean.

Those who aren't competing in the events can shop at swimsuit booths, play volleyball, or work on their tan. Besides being fun, these lifeguard events carry a serious message: protect our beaches and save our oceans.

"We want people to really treasure what is perhaps our greatest resource," says Hubbell. This is what southern California is all about.

Shauni McClain

Erika ELENIAK

Her pouty face, wheat-blonde hair and stunning figure could land Shauni McClain, voted most beautiful and most popular by her class, a lucrative modeling career. But Shauni, the epitome of what the Beach Boys meant when they sang, "I wish they all could be California girls", spends all her spare time at the beach. As well as being a California girl, Shauni is spoiled by her wealthy parents. She drives a flashy convertible, has a wardrobe full of the most fashionable — and sexiest — clothes, and rarely, if ever, hears the word "no". When she graduates from high school she decides she'd like to hang out down at the beach with her friends and get paid for it . . . by lifeguarding.

Growing up in California and having a huge and beautiful pool in her back yard gave Shauni excellent swimming skills. She has no trouble qualifying for rookie school. What she does have a problem with is wearing the regulation one-piece lifeguard swimsuit. The red swimsuit she chooses is so skimpy there is no room for the lifeguard patch! Shauni quickly finds she has eyes for co-rookie Eddie Kramer, but he is more than aloof.

After graduating rookie school, Shauni's main goal is to get a tower where she can be near her friends. Mitch's main goal is not to put her in a tower at all until he is sure she is ready. He teams her up with Jill Riley, a senior ocean guard. On their first day together, Shauni freezes on her first rescue. Jill has to administer CPR to an unconscious little girl as a weeping Shauni watches. Shauni quickly learns the hard way, with the help of Jill Riley, the true meaning of lifeguarding and the commitment she has to make. Shauni grows up fast, checks her snobby attitude at the door and takes her life and her lifeguarding career seriously.

Shauni has had several boyfriends, including a poet who wrote her love sonnets and set up a dancefloor, red roses and champagne next to her tower at the beach. She also had an abusive boyfriend who hit her. But Shauni learns the true meaning of love when she falls for fellow lifeguard Eddie Kramer. Her high-society parents do not approve of this Philly-bred ex-juvenile delinquent, and do whatever they can to stop the relationship from progressing. Shauni's father lets Eddie know point-blank that he doesn't approve of the relationship he is having with his daughter. Eddie saves Shauni's sister Kim from drowning when she tries to free her diamond engagement ring from the pool drain and gets stuck. When her parents still don't approve of Eddie, a frustrated Shauni resolves to leave home. Her parents threaten to cut her off, but Shauni calls their bluff by moving onto Eddie's houseboat with him.

Shauni and Eddie live, lifeguard and save lives together. When one of

Shauni's friends fakes her own death in a phony shark attack to get away from a controlling father and start a new life with her boyfriend, Shauni figures out what she has done and brings father and daughter together in an emotional reunion.

When an obese young girl develops a crush on Eddie and almost drowns because she is weak from crash dieting, Shauni takes her under her wing and helps her deal with her self-image. Being overweight, the girl feels she is judged by her appearance and that no one cares what is on the inside. A very emotional Shauni shares with the girl that she too has felt judged by her beautiful outward appearance, and that no one cares about her inner self either. She tells the girl how she overcame this, and they both realize that they have more in common than their feelings for Eddie.

People aren't the only creatures on the beach that need protection from the lifeguards. After rescuing a seal caught in a fishing net, Shauni

organizes a bikini contest to raise money for ORCAS, an aquatic rescue and rehabilitation organization that will have to shut down without the necessary funds. Mitch ends up helping her out, and ORCAS is saved.

While rafting white-water rapids with Mitch, CJ and Eddie, Shauni discovers she may be pregnant. She shares this news with Eddie, and when he proposes to her on the river bank with a reed fashioned into a ring, Shauni fears that her pregnancy may be the only reason Eddie wants to marry her. But when she finds out she isn't pregnant after all, Eddie, after saving her from the clutches of murderous mountain men, professes his undying love for her.

Shauni and Eddie have a romantic wedding back on the beach in L.A. with all their lifeguard friends present, before leaving for Australia on a lifeguard exchange program.

Eddie Kramer

Billy WARLOCK

Billy Warlock on Eddie Kramer: "Eddie's really trusted and admired Mitch. He's one of the reasons Eddie hung in there to begin with. I just wish Mitch had given Eddie some advice about getting married. Looking back, I think Eddie and Shauni got together too soon. They were way too young to get married. Once they moved to Australia it was an uphill battle, and they grew apart and ended up divorced. Eddie never had a chance to sow his wild oats, and he should have so that he could appreciate the good that comes to his life. Growing up in foster homes, Eddie didn't have that much love or stability in his life."

Dark, good-looking, brooding Eddie Kramer joins Baywatch rookie school, and the family he never had. He says his last name might as well have been Foster, considering how many foster homes he lived in as a kid. Mitch becomes his father figure, and Shauni soon becomes his girlfriend.

When Jimmy, an old buddy of Eddie's from his wild Philly days, shows up causing havoc, Eddie doesn't want anything to do with him. Sadistic Jimmy trips Eddie on his way to a rescue and, hothead that he is, Eddie decks Jimmy with his lifeguard can. Jimmy presses charges and Eddie is suspended. But Jimmy doesn't stop there. He torches Eddie's lifeguard tower . . . after he has locked Eddie and Shauni inside. Eddie saves himself and Shauni when he crashes through the flaming tower and lands on the sand, with Shauni safely in his arms.

This isn't the only tight squeeze Eddie and Shauni find themselves in. Trapped together in an armored car that falls off the end of the pier, Eddie is pinned to the floor under the heavy safe. When the car fills with water, quickly covering Eddie's head, Shauni has to give Eddie oxygen underwater via mouth-to-mouth, keeping him alive until they are rescued.

Eddie rescues Caroline, a young girl who decides the only way to gain acceptance from the popular girls at high

school is to say that she is having an affair with Eddie. When her strict father
finds out that she slept with a lifeguard, he charges Eddie with statutory
rape. Shocked to hear such a lie, Eddie is more shocked when he is
suspended from lifeguarding. Shauni, who stands by her man, not believing a
word of it, doesn't rest until she tracks Caroline down, getting her to admit
her lie and clear Eddie's name.

The only part of Eddie's past he doesn't mind being reminded of is his
brother Bobby. Eddie misses him terribly, and confides in Shauni that
Bobby lives on a horse ranch with a doctor and other kids like him. He is a
schizophrenic. Eddie asks Shauni to visit his brother with him. Bobby is
lovable and endearing and wants to visit Eddie. The doctor agrees, but when
Bobby continues to hear voices – a part of his illness – and falls off the pier,
Eddie realizes it is not safe for Bobby to live away from the horse ranch.

It breaks his heart, but he takes Bobby home, knowing this is where he
will be safe. When Eddie leaves town with Shauni after their wedding, he
vows to return one day to Baywatch, his true family.

Lifeguarding
on Baywatch

The American Red Cross awarded Baywatch the 1995 Spirit Award for demonstrating commitment to public education and the importance of water safety and cardio-pulmonary resuscitation. Baywatch depicts correct, constantly updated, techniques for life saving, and lives have been saved by viewers who have watched rescue and CPR techniques on Baywatch and then performed them in emergencies.

Whether the rescues on Baywatch involve victims trapped inside motorcycles and cars that have fallen off cliffs into the water, dislodging a piece of candy from a boy's throat before administering CPR, the use of a defibrillator when the victim has no pulse, people marooned on rocks out in the water, boat explosions at sea, victims caught in rip currents, people falling off piers or children knocked over by big waves, all rescue and CPR scenes are accurately depicted. There are always technical advisors on the set, whether they be lifeguards, paramedics or medical consultants, to oversee the correct procedures for all rescue techniques.

Baywatch has depicted rescues of animals as well as people. Among them dolphins, pelicans, seals, horses and dogs. From watching Baywatch, a child administered CPR to his rabbit after it fell into the swimming pool – and saved its life.

Baywatch is responsible for another type of rescue as well. Emotional rescues. After viewing the episode "Blindside", in which lifeguard John Cort loses his eyesight to a disease called retinitis pigmentosa, a teenage boy decided not to commit suicide. If his idol, Baywatch lifeguard John Cort,

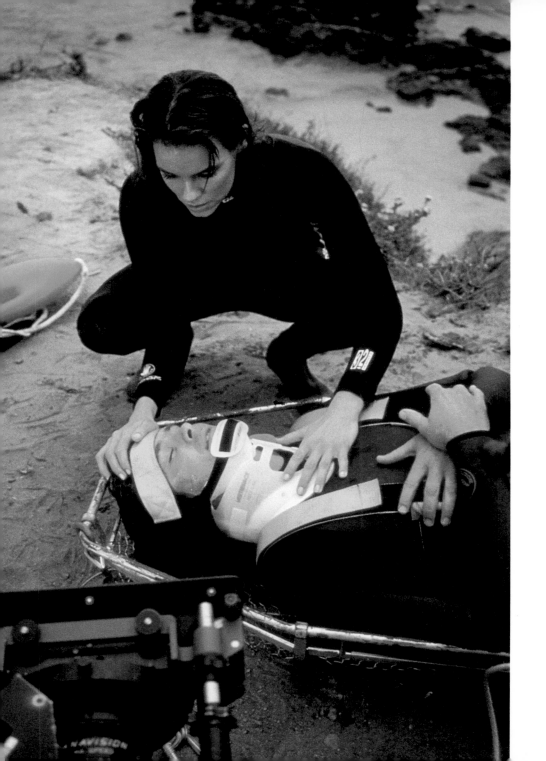

could handle the disease, so could he. This young man had kept his disability hidden. Now, because of Baywatch, he has the courage he needed to go on living. This was only one of thousands of responses to a public service announcement and phone number at the end of that episode.

In addition to blindness, other Baywatch episodes have depicted disorders and illnesses such as deafness, Down's syndrome, dwarfism, schizophrenia, AIDS, multiple personality disorder, obesity, Alzheimer's disease, skin cancer, bone marrow cancer, bulimia, paralysis and cystic fibrosis. These episodes have become wildly popular for their messages and their ability to prevent those suffering from these conditions from feeling abandoned and ignored, while at the same time educating the audience on various aspects of these disorders. Lives have been affected and changed forever in this, one of the most important rescues that could ever be made – understanding and acceptance of one's self.

Captain
Don Thorpe

Monte
MARKHAM

Monte Markham on Captain Don Thorpe: "Thorpe was a champion swimmer and diver and loved lifeguarding. But being a product of Los Angeles, he was caught up in the movie industry. He wasn't pursuing it, but he always thought someone, someday, somewhere might come up to him and say, 'Hey, let me put you on camera, I'll make you a star.' L.A. is a movie town, the center of the film industry, everyone is filming at the beach, there are movie stars, pool parties . . . it's seductive. Patroling the beaches, lifeguarding in his tower, pulling people out of the water, Thorpe was always thinking he could be the next Stallone, the next leading action hero. One day he turned around and realized he was Captain Thorpe headed for Chief, and that the dream was gone. It was never going to happen. When Thorpe gets a chance to live his dream coaching Mitch and Shauni when they're working on a scene for a new television show, he is in his element. He drives the director crazy as he stands by mouthing all the words of dialogue. He's great."

The most efficient, skilled, by-the-book lifeguard captain you would ever want to drive you crazy. That's how Mitch describes Captain Thorpe. Their relationship dates back to their Navy days together. Thorpe outranked Mitch then, too. He takes his career, and life in general, very seriously. He runs headquarters like he would run a navy sub: everything must be ship-shape and Bristol fashion. Not many people know, as Mitch

does, that deep down he's a kind-hearted softy. As Shauni would say, he hides it very well.

Thorpe loves to reminisce with Ben about the old days, and can't help but start his advice to new guards with "when I was in rookie school..." Thorpe's favorite technique for new guards is to hang out with them in their towers and show them the ropes. "Make us want to hang ourselves with one is more like it," Eddie Kramer would say.

When Thorpe's wife leaves him after twenty years of marriage, he shows up on Mitch's doorstep... with his suitcase. He just purchased a snazzy new red convertible sports car, and is ready to live the bachelor life with Mitch and Hobie. Needless to say, after a few days of Mitch's home being run like Baywatch headquarters, Mitch and Hobie's only goal in life is to get Thorpe and his wife back together again.

Thorpe finally gets the promotion he's always wanted and becomes Chief. But this means he will have to move downtown. For all he put them through, everyone at Baywatch headquarters is sad to see him go... kind of.

Kaye Morgan

Pamela BACH

Kaye Morgan, the daughter of a wealthy socialite from Pasadena, has spent her life seeing the realities of the rich and famous through the eyes of her father. After traveling the world and working on a novel, Kaye, now an investigative reporter, wants to seek out and report the realities of the poor and downtrodden. This doesn't sit well with her snobby father, which leads to friction between them. When Kaye comes to town and starts her own newspaper, the

Venice Voice, she meets handsome lifeguard Mitch Buchannon. Mitch and Kaye become good friends, always bordering on romance, but never quite getting there.

After the earthquake, a shaken-up Jackie Quinn sells

her beach hut, Jackie's Summer Place, and leaves California. The beach hut has been renamed the Sandy Cay Café, but no one knows who the new owner is until Kaye reveals that it is none other than herself, Kaye Morgan! Mitch is thrilled until Kaye allows DJ Larry Loomin' Large to promote his new radio station from her café. He offers a hundred-thousand-dollar prize to anyone who can figure out the answer to his riddle, the clues to which are scattered all over the beach. This brings hordes of people to the beach, putting great strain on the Baywatch guards who have to rescue people doing nutty things to find the clues and then conceal them from other treasure hunters. Seeing the danger in this situation, Kaye gives Larry the boot, but he sets up on the pier.

Kaye's true devotion lies in helping children. She knows sign language, and teaches a young deaf girl how to speak with her hands, introducing her to the world of communication through signing. When Nicholas Campbell, an eleven-year-old boy with leukemia, needs a bone marrow transplant, Kaye seeks out Mitch and Cort to find the boy's brother, the only possible donor. Kaye comforts the boy as he hovers near death, keeping his spirit alive until Mitch and Cort return with his brother. When Kaye gets involved with a group of blind children, she almost loses her life helping to save them from a deadly fire that breaks out in Malibu.

Rescue me

Boat RESCUES

Rescue boats, whether they be Scarabs – the largest boats in the lifeguard fleet – or inflatable boats, are used primarily to assist lifeguards during offshore emergencies. Each rescue boat carries two lifeguards and they may be deployed to help small boats in trouble, swimmers caught in a rip current being carried out to sea, surfers or windsurfers in distress, aircraft accidents in the water and any other number of emergencies. When the lifeguard dives off the boat to make the rescue, he will swim the victim back either to the boat or to shore, depending on the situation.

Helicopter RESCUES

The United States Coast Guards provide helicopter rescue. Helicopters are used to search for missing sailors or swimmers, and to transport critically injured victims to hospital. In most instances, the lifeguards will arrive on the scene before the helicopter. The lifeguards assist in the lift operation used to transfer the victim to the basket that is then hoisted into the helicopter.

Waverunner RESCUES

Wave runners, which resemble motor scooters in the water, are used for offshore rescues from lifeguard towers. Wave runners can get the lifeguard to the victim very quickly. A boat could not arrive as swiftly and, of course, swimming is much slower, especially if the victim is some distance out from the shore. A boogie board is attached to the back of the wave runner. When the lifeguard reaches his victim, he dives off the wave runner. The victim is placed on the boogie board and given CPR if necessary. The lifeguard drives the wave runner back to shore and completes treating the victim.

Emergency Beach Unit RESCUES

Emergency four-wheel drive units are used for various situations, emergency or non-emergency, such as severe first aid, backup for lifeguards, and crowd control. These units are equipped with a radio, resuscitator, oxygen, rescue cans, backboard, boat tow lines, and other rescue and emergency equipment. They are considered as mobile lifeguard towers and can cut across surface streets and right down on to the sand to assist lifeguards.

Swimming RESCUES

Swimming to the victim, diving if necessary to find him, and getting him safely to shore, administering CPR or any other first aid, is the most frequently used rescue technique.

Hovercraft

A hovercraft is used in rescue situations where time is critical, or the victim must be immobilized due to neck or back injuries. The hovercraft can go directly from the ocean, over the beach, to a waiting ambulance.

Submersions

A submerged victim is one who has disappeared beneath the surface of the water. Diving equipment is used, and search patterns can be organized based on water currents and surf conditions. Lifeguards can form a "human chain", searching downcurrent from the spot where the victim disappeared. Rescue boards may be used, as they provide good vantage points for the lifeguards and a platform for administering CPR once the victim is located.

John D. Cort

John Allen Nelson on John D. Cort: "Cort has a big handicap that has nothing to do with his bad eyesight. He adores women, and can't resist a pretty face. This weakness gets him into more trouble. Cort's a travellin' man, and for him there is a different girl in every port, and sometimes two or three. His fantasy would be to have a harem of women to fuss over him. And the ultimate harem would include CJ, Stephanie, Summer, Caroline and Neely . . . especially in an elevator. Can you imagine? Oh Lord!"

From the moment Mitch catches hunky, cocky, anything-goes John D. Cort hot-dogging on the sand astride a motorcycle with a beautiful blonde hanging on behind him, he knows his buddy has not changed at all. Cort has a hankering for breaking the rules, even though he sees it as mere bending. Best buddies, Cort and Mitch were navy seals before lifeguarding together. Cort got antsy and moved on, getting into trouble in as many ways as possible.

Putting his mercenary days behind him, Cort decides to come back to what he loves best . . . California and lifeguarding. He and Mitch pick up their close relationship as if no time has passed at all. Unfortunately, Cort alienates some of the other guards with his arrogant attitude. He clears out Eddie Kramer's locker because it was his years before. When Eddie protests, Cort decks him. But Mitch always overlooks Cort's faults, loving him as a true friend would, for the good and the bad.

Missing camaraderie with his best buddy, Cort convinces Mitch to enter a dune buggy race, Baja Run, with him. Cort neglects to tell Mitch that they will be smuggling Indian artifacts over the border in their buggy. When Mitch finds out he's been taken in by one of Cort's get-rich-quick schemes, he promptly takes Cort to the nearest Mexican orphanage, where he insists Cort leaves the artifacts. A reluctant Cort hands them over to the delighted nuns.

The next time Cort and Mitch go off on a mission together it is for a much more noble cause: they are trying to locate the brother of a young boy dying of bone cancer. The boy needs his brother for a lifesaving bone marrow transplant . . . and Cort risks his own life to find the brother.

Cort also has a profound effect on women. His hard-bodied physique, rippling abdominal muscles, bulging biceps, chiseled jaw, and sensual smile, set off by his cowboy hat and boots, get him any woman he wants. Luring a beautiful woman's dog to jump off her boat so that he can rescue the dog and bring it back to the arms of the oh-so-grateful babe is just Cort's style. His charm and looks never fail him. But when he set his sights on CJ Parker, he falls madly in love.

Much to CJ's dismay, Cort hits the road again. When he returns it's to stay and to reclaim his lifeguarding job at Baywatch, and CJ. He rides back into her life on his horse, Apache Warrior, lassoing a motorcycle rider who is hassling CJ on the sand, pulling him off his bike.

After finally deciding that what he wants from life is CJ and lifeguarding, Cort finds out he has a disease called retinitis pigmentosa and is slowly going blind. He knows he has to leave lifeguarding behind because of his failing vision, and he decides that he has to leave CJ behind as well. As he tells Mitch, "CJ deserves a man who is incurably romantic, not incurably blind." He breaks CJ's heart, and does not allow her to go with him as she wanted, riding off into the sunset on his horse.

When Cort comes back again, CJ is involved with Matt Brody. This time Cort is ready to make a commitment, but CJ professes her love for Matt and stays with him.

Jill Riley

Shawn WEATHERLY

Tall, blonde, athletic Jill Riley lives the competitive life of a volleyball player on the pro circuit. When she breaks up with her partner, she goes back to lifeguarding. Thrilled to have his friend return, Mitch welcomes Jill back to Baywatch as a senior ocean guard. There are some romantic sparks, and Jill always had a bit of a thing for Mitch. But she knows he is nursing a broken heart over his divorce and they never get past the good friends stage.

Bohemian in nature and an animal lover, Jill lives on a sailboat with her pet seal. When the seal swims away, she is more brokenhearted over losing him than she has been over any of the shattered love affairs she has suffered through the years.

Jill is a superb lifeguard devoted to her career of saving lives. The first time she holds a victim in her arms, it sends chills through her. She could make a difference... a difference as to whether someone lives or dies.

Nothing can equal that feeling for her,
and when she loses a victim, a man who
drowns during his routine morning
swim, Jill feels responsible. So much so
that she investigates the death herself
until she discovers that he was
murdered by a scuba-diving relative
after his inheritance.

Jill puts saving other people's lives
above her own. Saving three drowning
and terrified children who capsized in a
rubber boat proves to be her last rescue.
As she lifts the last child onto the
lifeguard scarab boat and into Shauni's
arms, she is attacked by a great white
shark, literally pulling her from Shauni's
grasp. Shauni screams in sheer horror as
she sees nothing but Jill's lifeguard can
trail off across the sea.

Jill's death sends shock waves
through Baywatch headquarters. All
the lifeguards gather together to pay
tribute to their friend in a lifeguard
funeral at sea.

Good vibrations

Surfing is more than just a sport, it is a way of life. "Surfing is interpreting nature and then acting in harmony with it. How do you harmonize with nature? The ocean dictates the policy, the surfer interprets that policy, bonds with it, plugs into it ... and they are in harmony," says Scott Hubbell. Surfing a wave is like living life. The surfer sits outside the breakers waiting for the perfect opportunity, the perfect wave. He may wait hours, watching set after set of waves roll by, until he has the timing down. Lying face down on his surfboard, arms in the water paddling, the surfer looks over his shoulder to place himself at the head of the wave, and stands up. Catching the wave of water under his board, the rest of the ride is up to the surfer. Yes, surfing is like life. The surfer has to work to catch the perfect wave. Once he is riding high on it, he will face different variables as the wave changes. If he is tuned in to the rhythms of the ocean, he will have an unbelievable experience. It's like a beautiful clean wall to draw on, but he has to design the approach ... just like life. If a wave breaks in front of the surfer, he might have to change direction in order to avoid a "wipe out", being knocked off his board. Once the surfer wipes out, there is no place to go except under tons of swirling sea water. But he has to make the judgment call: does he ride the wave all the way in and risk a wipe out, or does he pull out part way and try another wave?

A wave can be a way to express one's abilities to others, and the surfer uses the wave to this end. But if the surfer considers the wave to be an expression of nature, he merges with the wave, instead of using it. Hubbell sums it up. "A surfer has to interpret the ocean, its rhythms and its energies. He has to read the bible of nature and work with the waves in order to be successful. If he doesn't, he's gonna wipe out, just like life."

Surfers in the 1960s fell into three groups. There were the old-timers, the young California hot-doggers who were rebellious, and the newcomers who looked like surfers and wanted to be surfers, but weren't. This was a time when the Beach Boys wrote endless songs about surfing and surfer girls, and beach movies like "Gidget" and "Beach Blanket Bingo" were the rage. Everyone wanted to be a surfer, or look like one, drive a "woody" – a station wagon with wooden sides that holds surfboards – have an awesome surfboard, a surfer girlfriend with long blonde hair, and live the southern California surfer life. Following the cultural revolution of the 1960s, everyone yearned to get back to nature. This only made surfers, the real surfers, smile. They'd never left nature. How could they possibly get any closer to nature, bond any more tightly, than being encased in an ocean wave!

Surfing today is still a popular water sport. In addition, offshoots of surfing – body surfing and boogie boarding – have become the rage. Body surfing needs no equipment. You catch a wave with your head down and hold your breath for as long as possible. With both arms out in front of you, the object is to stay ahead of the wave and let it push you to shore. The bigger the wave, the longer you will have to hold your breath. Body surfers call this type of wave a "Lung Buster".

Boogie boarding is basically body surfing while lying on top of a board, approximately three-and-a-half feet long, made of styrofoam with a plastic coating. These boards are curled at the "nose", or the front, so that they glide across the wave. A wrist strap connects the board to the surfer so that it doesn't take off with the currents if you fall off. The idea behind boogie boarding is much the same as body surfing. Catch a great wave that takes you to shore – only you don't have to hold your breath boogie boarding!

Longboard surfing has come back into style and is one of the hottest beach sports around. These boards are much easier to surf because of their size and increased flotation. Competitors literally dance on the water on boards that are nine feet or longer. Longboarding events in southern California attract the top longboard surfers in the world. But it's not just for champs and young people – parents and kids often compete in the same

tournament and there are divisions for those fifty and older. Surfing is a great way for families to enjoy the beach together. There is no finish line for surfing competitions, rather the top four waves are scored by a panel of five judges and a head judge. The judges look for size of the waves, how much action the surfer gets in the best part of the wave, and style.

Surfing in southern California is a year-round activity. It doesn't matter to the surfers if it's sunny, windy, foggy or stormy. Different weather conditions make for different waves and a surfer will simply put on a wet suit if it's cold, rising to the challenge of nature. So whether they are surfing huge waves, sitting on glassy water waiting for a set of waves, walking the nose, hanging ten or shooting the curl, whether they be on a longboard or a shortboard, surfers are in their element. This sense of freedom to be with nature, to be in the warm California sun and sea, to be tan, blond and carefree, draws people from all over the world like magnets to this lifestyle . . . the fantasy lifestyle, simple as it may be, that these southern California surfers live every day.

California's greatest surfing spots include Malibu Surfrider beach, Black's beach in San Diego, Bluff Cove in Palos Verdes, often called "California's little Waikiki", and Hermosa beach.

Kelly Slater, who portrayed young surfer Jimmy Slade on Baywatch, holds the title of "Number One Surfer in the World". At the age of twenty-two, he is the youngest surfer to hold this title. While working on Baywatch, his focus was split and he lost the title. After leaving Baywatch, he concentrated full time on his surfing and reclaimed the number one position.

Trevor Cole

His card reads "shark fighter and virgin converter", and he claims he's lost a few battles... but only to the sharks. This is how Trevor Cole introduces himself to Mitch Buchannon and Jill Riley when he shimmies up the fireman's pole into Baywatch headquarters.

This cocky Australian came to lifeguard in the States, but since he is not a trained L.A. county guard, he gets a job at the neighboring beach club which does not require county certification. Because of this, the Baywatch guards consider him as "not being there", and watch his water as well.

During a blitz rescue, Mitch catches Trevor passing up a drowning victim to save a beautiful girl. Mitch chews him out, requesting quite strongly that Trevor does not allow such an incident to occur again or he will have Mitch to answer to. Due to his cocky attitude and sub-standard lifeguarding practices, Trevor is not winning any popularity contests with the Baywatch guards.

When he almost loses a victim to secondary drowning – lungs flooding with body fluids as a result of swallowing too much sea water – Trevor decides he needs to attend rookie school and become a county certified guard. Trevor passes the qualifying

swim but Mitch almost boots him
out of rookie school the first day
because of his bad attitude. When
an exhausted Treyor is offered
steroids by Jeff, a fellow rookie, he
turns him down, promising he
won't narc on him. During a rookie
school running exercise, Jeff
collapses. When it is determined
that he suffered a heart attack,
everyone is shocked except Trevor.
He knows it was steroid induced.

Trevor goes to see Mitch,
realizing he should have turned
Jeff in as well as turning him down.
Trevor tells Mitch he wants to
resign. Knowing there is no love
lost between them, Trevor is
surprised when Mitch won't accept
his resignation. He tells Trevor
he knows they don't see eye to eye,
but it took guts to come forward,
and he respects that. Maybe he'll
make an okay county guard
after all.

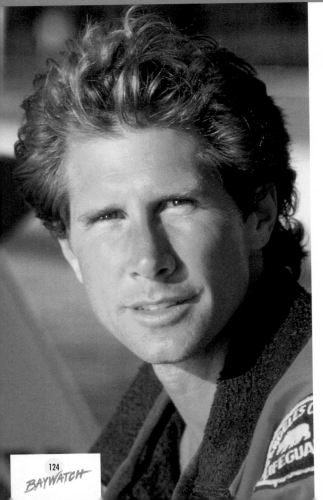

Craig Pomeroy

Parker STEVENSON

Many lifeguards have other careers. They are firemen, doctors or businessmen. They simply can't give up lifeguarding ... it's in their blood. Craig Pomeroy is a lawyer who just can't give up the feel of sand in his toes. He keeps a box of sand under his desk at his law practice and wriggles his bare feet through the sand so that he can think. His boss thinks he has to make a decision; he's a lawyer now and has to give up lifeguarding. He can't be both. Craig doesn't agree. He worked hard to become a lawyer, but he'll always be a lifeguard.

Craig adores his wife Gina, whom he met during a trial when she was a witness. During cross-examination, Craig says he couldn't trip her up or pin her down, so he married her. Gina would like to give Craig one other job description ... father. She wants to have a baby and is always setting up romantic evenings or getaways so that they have time to make their baby. That's Craig's problem and Gina's major beef – with two careers, he has no time to spare.

Craig rescues a teenage girl, Laurie, when she falls off the pier, and she becomes infatuated with her hero. Her infatuation soon turns into obsession and she tells everyone, including Gina, that Craig made love to her in his lifeguard tower. This obsession becomes worse when Laurie tries to kill Gina. Craig is able to save Gina from Laurie's sick mind, and get Laurie the help she needs.

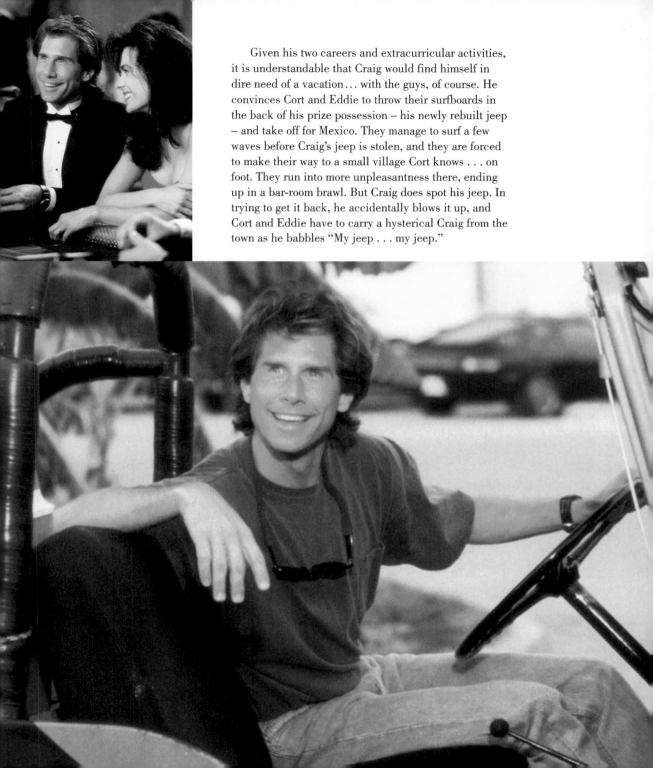

Given his two careers and extracurricular activities, it is understandable that Craig would find himself in dire need of a vacation... with the guys, of course. He convinces Cort and Eddie to throw their surfboards in the back of his prize possession – his newly rebuilt jeep – and take off for Mexico. They manage to surf a few waves before Craig's jeep is stolen, and they are forced to make their way to a small village Cort knows . . . on foot. They run into more unpleasantness there, ending up in a bar-room brawl. But Craig does spot his jeep. In trying to get it back, he accidentally blows it up, and Cort and Eddie have to carry a hysterical Craig from the town as he babbles "My jeep . . . my jeep."

Junior lifeguards

Where do lifeguards come from? A great many of them come from high-school swim teams. But according to Michael Newman, the most valuable training tool is the junior lifeguard program. This program takes place every summer along the beaches of southern California. It is not expensive to enter the program and only a timed swim test is necessary to qualify. The program is every day for four hours, five days a week, for six weeks. There is a great deal to learn about the ocean and this is the best place to obtain that knowledge.

In addition, there are many physical demands. Swimming out into the ocean around buoys, running on the beach, simulated rescues, the learning of CPR and other rescue techniques, pier jumps, jumping off the back of a moving boat and swimming to shore... in fact, anything a real lifeguard needs to be able to do.

At the end of the program there is a junior lifeguard competition with events much like the regular lifeguard competitions. The different beaches form teams and compete against one another in various beach events – once again, just like the real lifeguards. According to Newman, "There is nothing better than seeing a top junior lifeguard finish the rookie test. It's great."